The Great British
Entrepreneur's
Handbook 2014

eBook edition

As a buyer of the print edition of *The Great British Entrepreneur's Handbook* you can download the eBook edition free of charge to read on an eReader, smartphone, tablet or computer. Simply go to:

ebooks.harriman-house.com/gbehandbook

Or point your smartphone at the QRC code above.

You can then register and download your free eBook.

Follow us on Twitter – **@harrimanhouse** – for the latest on new titles and special offers.

www.harriman-house.com

 Harriman House

The Great British Entrepreneur's Handbook 2014

Inspiring entrepreneurs

HARRIMAN HOUSE LTD
3A Penns Road
Petersfield
Hampshire
GU32 2EW
GREAT BRITAIN
Tel: +44 (0)1730 233870

Email: enquiries@harriman-house.com
Website: www.harriman-house.com

First published in Great Britain in 2013.
Each chapter remains copyright © of the respective author.

The right of the authors to be identified as the Authors has been asserted in accordance with the Copyright, Designs and Patents Act 1988.

ISBN: 9780857193704

British Library Cataloguing in Publication Data
A CIP catalogue record for this book can be obtained from the British Library.

FURTHER LEGAL INFORMATION

GUY RIGBY

Disclaimer

By necessity this briefing can only provide a short overview and it is essential to seek professional advice before applying the contents of this article. No responsibility can be taken for any loss arising from action taken or refrained from on the basis of this publication. Article correct at time of writing.

Smith & Williamson LLP

Regulated by the Institute of Chartered Accountants in England and Wales for a range of investment business activities. A member of Nexia International.

SUSAN PERRY

The contents of this chapter are intended for general information purposes only and shall not be deemed to be, or constitute legal advice. Neither the author nor Kerman & Co LLP can accept responsibility for any loss as a result of acts or omissions taken in respect of this chapter.

Foreword

ENTREPRENEURS ARE THE lifeblood of the economy.

The intention of the *Great British Entrepreneur's Handbook* is to share the wisdom of experienced entrepreneurs on topics that are close to their hearts and businesses. Each has a wealth of knowledge, grown over years of entrepreneurial successes and failures, and we are grateful for their contributions.

Entrepreneurs, by their very nature, are businesses' biggest risk-takers and have a drive that is rare in the corporate world. Forever seeking a way to reach for the stars, they will take chances and accept potential failures with a resilience that speaks volumes of their characters. Being an entrepreneur is as much about a personality as it is about a business model.

As a business community, we have talked a lot about why entrepreneurs are important in the UK, but we have done very little to genuinely acknowledge their achievements. The Great British Entrepreneur Awards are here to celebrate entrepreneurs and recognise their success amongst their peers. This *Handbook* hopes to be part of this by sharing some of the exclusive and hard-won insights of a number of top entrepreneurs working today.

The triumphs of the British entrepreneurial community are vast and varied and we are delighted to be a part of the awards that are set to become a benchmark for entrepreneurial success in the future.

Thank you for your support – we hope you enjoy reading.

GREAT BRITISH
ENTREPRENEUR
AWARDS 2013

In association with

Contents

The Power of Live

by Simon Burton

IT'S EASY TO forget in our digital world that the nature of human communication has always been social; the great moments of our lives have been shared in communities; and the 'know *who*' of network has always been as important as the 'know how'.

Social media is a fantastic enhancement to these basic human relationships but it is no replacement. People the world over have been shaking hands to greet one another and seal the deal for over 2,500 years. Over 93% of communication is non-verbal, so body language, tone of voice, personal presentation and environment are all more important in terms of meaning and understanding than any words exchanged.

Face-to-face communication is the most powerful, underrated and underused tool in the entrepreneur's armoury, but it's a skill we risk under-exploiting in the digital age.

Entrepreneurs have networking hardwired into their DNA. They are natural connectors and natural sharers of ideas. Most of all the passion and desire that burns within them means they are on a constant quest to find someone who will listen to them talk about their fantastic business or share the pain of the 'slings and arrows' of commercial misfortune. Entrepreneurs are evangelists.

In the midst of the modern technological revolution, television has provided another illustration of how powerful face-to-face presentation is. Television has excited us about the pitch again. Now it's not just something ad agencies do; pitching is a basic unit of currency whenever we are trying to sell anything, be it idea, product, service or vision of the future. In our new digital and connected world television is an old medium, but it is an extraordinary instrument that has shown us all the power of presenting to potential investors. And once we become viewers rather than participants, it's all too easy to see that the quality of the idea is much less important than the quality and charisma of the presentation.

It's great that TV has become interested in business and entrepreneurs and it's great that the wider public is increasingly seeing entrepreneurs as powerful tools for change and forces for good. Some of this is partly because TV captures the drama of the pitch, business challenge or boardroom and partly because the entrepreneurs' personalities and passions shine through. We're rooting for them and for us to root for someone they need to have charisma.

Whilst all this is great – entrepreneurs should be seen as heroes – screens don't capture the nuances or subtleties of an actual meeting and all the evidence from marketers and business people is that we instinctively and empirically know that face to face works best. We want to get that meeting. We want to get 'in front' of a client. The entrepreneurs want to present their idea face to face, not through the distortion of a screen.

Research shows that over 90% of marketers and business directors believe that face-to-face marketing is the most effective media channel to convert prospects. But it's not just about closing the deal that gives face to face its power. Relationships matter in business and all the stats point to the same thing: face-to-face relationships last longer and have higher transactional value. Real-world relationships are longer lasting, better quality and worth more than relationships forged elsewhere. But that's obvious isn't it? Most of us would want to actually meet a potential partner from a dating site before we marry them.

One of the trends of modern business life is to retreat behind email. It's a move we make at our peril. We need to speak, to engage, to connect, to meet. Real relationships are more robust and meaningful than purely digital ones. There are two ways to make a connection: a digital 'click' that's devoid of profound meaning or the genuine 'click' that comes from the chemistry of meeting people. Chemistry with people is a vital part of our business personalities and lives. Given an even choice, we'll always do business with people whose company we enjoy. Personality, presentation, energy and charisma count for a great deal in ourselves, as well as our team.

But it's not an 'either/or'. The best real-life networkers frequently have huge numbers of online connections and regularly share their real-life experiences online. If you're well-turned-out and charming in real life then your website and online profiles should be well-turned-out and charming as well. Live plus digital is a very powerful cocktail. The basics of good business practice in the real world prevail in cyber space too. At their best the two work in tandem.

Trade shows are about as traditional and direct as face-to-face marketing gets and the perfect launchpad for many an entrepreneurial endeavour or a young business wanting to get its product to market. Visitors attend exhibitions specifically to look for new stuff. So, in the case of that buyer who won't return your call or ignores your emails, he or she will be at your industry trade show on the hunt for the new, the innovative and the undiscovered. This gives you the perfect opportunity to put your product straight into their hands. But for every tale of great trade show success, there's one of wasted budgets and frustration at unmet targets. All too frequently the reasons for a lack of success are nothing to do with the show itself.

So here's a sobering stat to make you rethink all the clever plans and amazing graphics for your exhibition stand; 80% of the effectiveness of your exhibition stand is due to the stand staff. Forget about position in the hall or being next to the seminar theatre, the single most important component in exhibition success is your people. It's probably one of the most important factors in any context, but, face to face, great people make a great deal of difference.

And as if that stat wasn't sobering enough, here's the double-espresso info: 70% of trade show leads never get followed up. Never. Not even a generic email or brochure. Nothing. The hottest leads in the world are left to go icy cold. Some of the world's greatest networkers and sales people aren't necessarily the best at the face-to-face part – but all of them are good at the follow-up part, turning that first connection into a meaningful business action.

Digital and social media in all its forms should make things easier. Easier to follow up, easier to connect online, easier to share experiences and information and, from a sales and marketing ROI standpoint, easier to measure outcomes. Social networks and real-life meetings at their best co-exist and enhance one another. Many of the most powerful networkers and relationship builders are also adept in their use of social media to capture and retain contacts, to update their networks and to create ongoing engagement and interaction. It's all about putting those components in the right order and recognising where priorities lie.

And that order is flexible and adaptable. In fact, some of social media's greatest successes are in the way it promotes and facilitates personal relationships. Want romance? Then dating sites will take you from an online picture to the love of your life. Want thousands of teenagers to come to a party at your house? Then publicise it on Facebook. Follow and engage with someone on Twitter and you can be certain that the conversation will flow more smoothly when you do meet. Profundity, durability and meaning in human relationships come from multiple connections in multiple environments with multiple touch points. The combination of real-life social events and digital world social media is a powerful cocktail to forge those relationships, make connections and share experiences.

It's perhaps the notion of shared experiences that is the most exciting way in which social media seamlessly entwines with real-world events. Experiences now extend way beyond the physical walls that confine an event. Football matches, royal weddings, talent shows and political rallies are now amplified and commented upon by millions via social media. We're all journalists, we're all broadcasters and we're all media owners; and in the constant quest for compelling content, events and experiences are a regular source of subject matter.

But great content isn't enough; great content needs powerful presentation, engaging storytelling and charismatic personality. If you're business is entirely 'tech' and you're operating purely in a world of data then you might be able to avoid the need to connect and engage, but for most of us the ability to tell your story and make people want to listen is what sets us apart. In a world with information overload only the brightest, most appealing information stands a chance of being seen or heard. Learning how to tell your story can be the most powerful tool you have. This is truly the era of the elevator pitch and you need to make sure that your pitch doesn't require a very tall building and a very slow elevator.

The digital revolution has created a whole new generation of entrepreneurs who have re-engineered broken business models, modernised outdated working methods and re-thought how we conduct some of the most fundamental aspects of our day-to-day lives. Disruption and thinking the unthinkable are the orders of the day. Social media and the virtual world have co-opted the language of relationship – "connection", "like", "share", "recommend", "community" – and they add enormously to the process of relationship building. But the real manifestation of relationship will always be in the real world.

In a world of screens, face to face has never been more powerful.

Simon Burton is founder of
the Great British Entrepreneur Awards.

WWW.GREATBRITISHENTREPRENEURAWARDS.COM

The Five Kinds of Entrepreneur

by Ewan MacLeod

YOU KNOW WHAT? We need more entrepreneurs. Because they're the lifeblood of our economy, sure – but also because they foster the kind of creativity and innovation that Britons are famous for the world over.

Working on Bizcrowd has given me the opportunity to meet a dazzling array of entrepreneurial talent. Britain's small businesses come in all shapes and sizes and are born out of all kinds of circumstances – but I'm starting to get a feel for a few distinct 'tribes' among them. Five, to be precise. I call them The Advisor, The Salesperson, The Diplomat, The Creator and The Doer. Which one are you?

The Advisor

If you're an Advisor – also known as the problem-solver – you handle a crisis in a calm, secure way. You are also a skilled communicator; everyone you know, and I mean everyone, wants your advice. You're comfortable in work that demands lucid decision-making no matter how chaotic the situation, and you are brilliant at designing processes.

Some people just are brilliant at process. Henry Ford is an obvious example, having pretty much invented the modern production line. I know, I know. Process doesn't sound sexy. But at the end of the day, it's what turns great ideas into actual profits. And everything you can do in your production process to save costs or bundle in extra features builds value.

So go on, fly your analytical flag with pride!

Your key strengths are: strategy, attention to detail, getting the most out of your people.

The Salesperson

Ah, Sales Guy. Though you are sometimes maligned, when you're truly good at what you do, you're a joy to behold. You come alive in a crowd and at networking events. If making small talk was a competitive sport, you'd be in the Olympics. Which makes sense, because this type of entrepreneur is an adventurer. While money is important to you, it's really the excitement of execution that gets your blood going – and when that's not enough, you probably put your life in danger in some other way. Let me guess – parachute jumping? The scariest ski slope you can find? Deep-sea diving, perhaps?

The Salesperson may boast crossover traits with other entrepreneurial categories, but they're primarily adrenaline junkies who you couldn't pay to give up their 'fix'.

Your key strengths are: energy, tenacity, a 'work hard / play hard' culture.

The Diplomat

The Diplomat is politically astute to an extraordinary level. A natural mediator who can negotiate the impossible, this entrepreneur can somehow infiltrate bureaucracies and make them sing. Above all, the Diplomat is a skilled opportunist, looking for ways to use the existing system to their advantage. Charming and dynamic, they think big and often find the 'thing' of the moment.

If this is you, you are also likely to be extremely flexible and comfortable with change, making you a serial innovator who moves happily on to pastures new when new opportunities present themselves. Easy come, easy go, Diplomat!

Your key strengths are: spotting gaps, speed of execution, infiltrating other companies and systems and influencing them.

The Creator or Visionary

People who aren't in business sometimes think all entrepreneurs are Creators, but I don't think that's true. This is you if you crave variety with sophisticated strategy and always have the big picture in focus. Alas, the thought of balancing your cheque book fills you with dread, as you bore easily. Very, very easily.

Creators are driven by a desire to change the world – and the capacity to imagine how to do so. Of course, vision on its own is just daydreaming, so such an entrepreneur needs other skills to bring their vision to life. Quite often Creators are brilliant at recruiting other brilliant people and sharing the delivery of the vision with them. That's the beauty of being a big-picture person.

Your key strengths are: your imagination, seeing the big picture, realising your limitations and delegating to brilliant followers.

The Doer

Doers are often 'detail' people with a particular specialism. You're industrious, disciplined and dependable. With your tenacity and organisational skills, you could run your own small country. You may even feel that you have a calling, or that you were born to do what you do.

The world is full of doers who turn their special aptitude and natural affinity for a certain product, service or field into something we all rely on. You tend not to over-think things. Of all the entrepreneurial types, you are the least likely to have delusions of grandeur, and because of this you often forge ahead. You just roll up your sleeves and get on with it. Thank goodness for you.

Your key strengths are: your self-knowledge, dedication, the ability to be self-motivated and just get on with it.

So there you are – my five entrepreneurial tribes! Did you recognise yourself in any of them? If you forced me to pick a category for myself, I'd probably select the Advisor as I do like pointing out the way ahead with friends and colleagues and I'm good at designing the 'how'.

Or perhaps the Doer, because I've often had no option but to muck in at the front line when there's simply no one else to do what needs to be done.

More often than not, I've felt the urge to become a Creator and create things from scratch. Indeed, I was so annoyed with the 'can't be done' message coming from my developers that I spent one Christmas holiday teaching myself to write PHP web code so that I could make a product come to life.

The more I think about it, though – and the more businesses I've founded – the more I recognise that a successful entrepreneur could and probably should exhibit traits from all five of these profiles. I think the challenge is cultivating the behaviours that aren't natural strengths – and, of course, knowing when to switch.

To all you entrepreneurs out there: happy strategising, innovating and organising. And please come and see us at **Bizcrowd.com**.

Ewan MacLeod is Head of Bizcrowd.

WWW.BIZCROWD.COM

Getting Greatness From Your Employees

by Eugene Kaspersky

IN THE SPRING of 2013 the Tolbachik volcano on the Kamchatka Peninsula became active, after having woken from a long sleep at the end of 2012. So what's that got to do with business at Kaspersky Lab, you might ask. Well, it doesn't affect KL at all, but that's the point. Confused? Let me explain …

As a hardcore devotee of exotic and extreme travel, and having a particular fondness for all things volcanic, when I first heard the news about Tolbachik I decided there and then that I had to get myself over there to see it in the flesh. After all, Tolbachik blowing its top only occurs once in a blue moon (the last time was in the mid-70s). So I dropped everything and flew off to Kamchatka later that day. The next day I was stood right next to a crack in the volcano's crater and observing the lava flow. Meanwhile back at Kaspersky Lab, it was just another working day, all systems go, as if its CEO was still sat in his office.

The system of management at Kaspersky Lab is set up in such a way that I don't need to interfere in its workings every day. I look for the right people and distribute tasks appropriately so that I don't need to keep track of how everything's going. I don't get bogged down in details. I rarely ever sign papers – only when I really have to. But that's OK as I've issued powers of attorney to all the key senior managers. One thing I know for sure is that if I did get into the nitty gritty of details – and for a firm the size of KL that's a lot of details – then nothing good would come of it. I'd burn myself out at the same time too. Instead, I operate at KL in a flexible and as-and-when fashion, focusing on particular issues that actually would do well in having my direct input on them. Otherwise, if it ain't broke, don't fix it.

Back before KL was founded I came up with a single guiding rule for how I should conduct myself professionally (and not long ago I read somewhere that Richard Branson established the same rule for himself): To find the right people, trust them, and give them freedom to act. I have always asked the same from my managers too: that they in turn find the right team members and give them freedom based on trust. And who are the right people? Those whose main motivator is professional interest – for example, the complexity and originality of the tasks at hand; while remuneration comes from successfully solving those tasks. When you trust folks, they're happier. When you control constantly, they stop taking decisions and lose a sense of responsibility over what they do.

The win-win for me in giving people freedom to act is that, well, I don't have to spend time – lots of it – looking over folks' shoulders. Just as well, since I've always had enough work to be getting on with as it is. Let me give you a few examples of how.

Around the late 1990s and early 2000s I worked on a task that was vital for the survival of the company – maintaining the quality of technologies. No quality – no business. We'd created the world's best antivirus engine and started licensing it out, with business partners appearing fast. I then started preparing and signing contracts, but quickly got tired of that. Thus, the company needed a general director – so that I could get back to fiddling with technologies. But we didn't have enough money to pay one! So my then-wife took on the day-to-day management responsibilities. Then, in 2003–05, I switched over to product development. I didn't write the code myself – I just oversaw and monitored the work of the teams working on 'breakthrough' products. At this time I also retired from antivirus research after ushering in a new generation of experts who could do this work better than me.

I've always taken part in all key strategic decisions of the company. It's in operational management I've become less and less involved. So it was logical that I became KL CEO in 2007. At that time we set ourselves an ambitious goal – to be among the top-three world leaders of the antivirus market in three years. To reach that goal a few changes were needed in terms of both the team and structure of the company, or more precisely – zones of responsibility. Since then the structure of the company has significantly altered quite a few times. I think of it as soup. For the soup to come out good, it needs a good stirring.

Naturally, we sometimes suffer some mess-ups. Only in February 2013 we had some problems with a product. Turned out it wasn't a programmer's mistake but a systemic one. We were thus forced to make a few adjustments: to adjust zones of responsibility, and to do a bit of reshuffling to get some folks into more suitable positions. Sometimes foul-ups lead to some folks getting fired, but this time we didn't resort to that; the goof was the first of its kind. At KL we have a rule: don't make the same mistake twice. If you do, it's goodbye. To make different mistakes once – that's fine. It's impossible not to make some mistakes when you're creating something new and solving new problems. I myself make mistakes, always have, always will; and I keep telling others: keep trying and don't be afraid of the odd slip-up!

Anyway, back to my rule of giving the troops freedom to act, based on trust: how does it work? First off, it doesn't mean anarchy; if it did we'd stop applying the rule. How it works is by leaving the 'how' of getting to predetermined common goals to the people in the various working roles actually doing the various tasks involved. A member of the team might combine several roles, or a role may sometimes be spread among several individuals. As I see it, in organising any project there are normally seven main roles that can reside behind a number of different titles. These fundamental roles are as follows:

1. The architect (the one who sees the whole picture of the creation of a product, controlling the development from start to finish).

2. The investor (the one who promotes the project to the management of the company, secures the budget, and creates the right conditions for a smooth and fruitful team effort).

3. The technical designer (the one who knows how and how *not* to put into practice the ideas of the architect).

4. The product manager (the product needs to meet the demands of the customer, and this individual is the one who brings product and customer together).

5. The project manager (who keeps on top of deadlines, maintains the tempo of the work, and if necessary administers kicks up backsides).

6. The psychologist (a very important and often underrated role: to oversee the microclimate in the team and solve any conflicts).

7. The documenter (another important and sometimes overlooked role: this person documents each step in the chain

of work processes – to be clear on reasons for any mistakes, which, as you'll recall, cannot be repeated!).

Of course, accounting keeps track of things, including a system for the collection and recording of information on current projects. I get regular reports, but hardly daily ones. I normally just go by how wide the CFO's smile is! You'd be surprised at how accurate it is. I can check on financial matters at any moment, but hardly need to, since if there's something up those in charge will be the first to know about it and will be dealing with it effectively. I don't even ask for a report on mistakes – as long as they're corrected.

But my laissez-faire has its limits. Everyone in the company knows that I can approach anyone at any time to get information on this or that aspect of work. There's a clause on it in the charter! It's basically my keeping tabs on what I see as the very most important things that make up the wider picture. And they change all the time. I can wake up one morning and want to look at how things are doing in this or that respect. The next day – something totally different. But this roving overview never involves summoning anyone to my office. I always go see the respective people at their working place, have a chat, and a get a good look and feel of the matter.

Of course, sometimes I might not be in the office, or in Moscow, or even in Russia (half of my working time I spend on business trips all around the world speaking at conferences, attending exhibitions, conducting negotiations, and meeting partners). But that in no way affects the work of KL: roles have been determined, the appropriate authorities distributed. An apotheosis of this: when I say to someone at work: "We need to do that this way," and the reply comes: "We've been doing that for a week already!"

I understand that at some point in the future I'll need to move away from management completely and my place will be taken by someone else. It's most likely that with him or her running things the company will change. But I'm fine with that. If the person who replaces me wants to change something, that's their right. The main thing will be my being able to trust them – completely. No half measures. As Ralph Waldo Emerson put it: "Trust men and they will be true to you; treat them greatly and they will show themselves great."

Eugene Kaspersky is Chairman and CEO of Kaspersky Lab.

WWW.KASPERSKY.COM

Break the Rules

by Rachel Bridge

WHEN SCOTT ABBOTT and Chris Haney invented the board game *Trivial Pursuit* they initially only managed to raise enough money to make 1,100 sets of the game, which meant that each set cost them $75 to manufacture. However, they had to sell it to retailers for just $15 so that the retailers could sell it on to customers for $29.95 – itself a huge amount to pay for a board game at the time – meaning that they were selling each game at a $60 loss.

Even when they were able to make 20,000 copies for their second production run they knew that even if they managed to sell all 20,000 they would barely break even. Worse still, few people had any interest in buying the game.

Many people would probably, and understandably, have given up at this stage.

But the two of them did not give up. They spent three years trudging round sales fairs, shopping malls, and even doing home demonstrations trying to drum up interest in *Trivial Pursuit*. It was really hard work trying to persuade anyone to stock it, and even harder trying to find someone willing to distribute their game for them.

It was not the most sensible or obvious way to start a business. The first rule of enterprise is, after all, that you must sell your product for more than it costs you to make, in order to generate a profit. And the second rule is that you must sell something that people actually want to buy. But their determination eventually paid off. Scott and Chris finally managed to get a distributor to take on their game and within two years the game was a massive hit, at one point selling 20 million copies a year. *Trivial Pursuit* has now sold more than 88 million copies around the world and in 2008 games company Hasbro, which had been making the game under licence, paid $80 million to buy the rights to the game, making the two creators very rich indeed.

One of the most compelling reasons to start a business is knowing that this is the one area in life where you really can do it your way. There are few areas in life where you can genuinely tread in untouched snow but, happily, starting a business is one of them. No, it makes no sense to sell a product at a huge loss. And it makes even less sense to try and sell something that nobody wants. But sometimes someone will succeed by doing exactly that, and by doing a hundred other things that are on the face of it wrong and foolish too. Rules are not there to be blindly followed, they are there to guide and to suggest – and then possibly to completely ignore. The thing is, you are not at school anymore. You really can do what you want. And that is what makes entrepreneurship so very exciting.

The buzz word in successful entrepreneurship right now is 'disruptive', and although it sounds a bit too much like a bunch of naughty five-year-olds pouring paint on the carpet for my liking, the fact is that the start-up businesses which explode into a stagnant market like a crazy firework and turn every received wisdom on its head are often incredibly successful – and very exciting to watch. The traditional car-hire market was trundling along fairly aimlessly, until Streetcar came along to disrupt the market with its new model of accessible car clubs offering hire by the hour for busy professionals who didn't want the hassle of owning their own car. It worked, too – in 2010 Streetcar was sold to US firm Zipcar for £32.4 million.

And the banking market is currently being turned on its head by brash newcomers such as Metrobank, as well as alternative funders such as Funding Circle and Crowdcube, who are all offering customers a different way of meeting their needs.

When Victoria Barnsley started her publishing company Fourth Estate at the age of 29 she admits she had no idea what she was doing. Her father would beg her to give it up and get a proper job for fear that she would lose lots of money. However, Victoria soon found that the big advantage of being a newcomer to the industry was that it meant she was free to do things her own way.

When she produced a book with a white cover everyone told her she couldn't do that because no one ever bought books with white covers. But she ignored them and published it – and it was such a success that soon everyone else started publishing books with white covers too.

As Victoria says: "To start with we broke the rules because we didn't know the rules. Then we got a bit cheeky and realised we enjoyed breaking the rules. I learned that there is no one way of doing things."

And one of her biggest successes came about as a direct result of breaking the rules, when she decided to publish a very short book called *Longitude* by Dava Sobel. The book had already been turned down by many well-established publishers who thought no one would ever buy a book on such an obscure scientific subject – and they would certainly never buy a book with so few pages. Victoria decided to publish it regardless. It shot straight to number one on the bestseller list and has since sold hundreds of thousands of copies.

Never let anyone tell you that something can't be done. And never catch yourself saying it to anyone else, either. The most important questions an entrepreneur can ask are: 'Why?' 'Why not?' 'Why is it done this way?' 'Why not this way?' Then you just need to follow up with the magical sentence that begins: *Let's see what happens if…* '

The secret is to approach everything with a completely open mind, read as widely as you can and listen to as many people as you can. Then to feel free to ignore most of their advice and make your own mind up about things.

The fact is that many long-established rules for starting a business have simply been overtaken or rendered obsolete in the past few years by advances in technology, communications and simply the way the world works. Indeed I wrote my fourth book, *How to Make a Million Before Lunch*, because I realised that many of the established rules about starting and growing a business were simply a waste of time, a waste of money or even actively detrimental to the success of a fledgling business. The fact is, you don't actually need to invent a new product, or take on staff, or even have relevant experience or qualifications to start a business. Having the right attitude and a willingness to learn will see you though. And I wrote my fifth book, *How to Start a Business Without Any Money*, for the same reason – so many people were getting stuck on the outdated rule that insisted they needed a stack of money in order to start a business that they were being stopped in their tracks, their dreams left to die.

Anna Gibson and Philippa Gogarty are a wonderful example of two people who decided to rewrite the rulebook, to great success. As two full-time mothers with six young children between them, and zero experience of running a business, they were not the most obvious candidates to become the British distributors of micro-scooters, a three-wheeled scooter for children. Especially because they had no intention of putting their children in childcare or leaving them with nannies while they went to work five days a week in an office elsewhere. Instead they found ways of working in the small pockets of time squeezed in around looking after their children.

Anna says:

> "We would work for three hours in the morning when the youngest ones were at nursery and then we would work till 2am in the morning every night once the children had gone to bed. We were always there at the school gate to pick them up. I remember talking to a shipping agent when we were in Philippa's kitchen trying to give Marmite sandwiches to six children at the same time as trying to find out how much it cost to ship a pallet from Germany."

Despite the seeming impossibility of managing to be around for their children and also build a serious business at the same time, they managed it brilliantly, and their business now has a multi-million pound turnover.

Judy Craymer broke the rules even more spectacularly. When she decided to write a musical based on the songs of Abba everyone thought she was doubly crazy – firstly because at the time Abba's music was deeply unfashionable and something people would never admit to liking, and secondly because no one ever made money out of musicals. But Judy decided to ignore all the naysayers and plough ahead regardless. In the end it took her ten years to get her project off the ground. Along the way she had to sell her flat to fund the costs she was incurring, even before she had managed to get formal permission from Björn Ulvaeus and Benny Andersson, the members of Abba who had written the songs, to let her use them.

But she persisted. And just look at her now. Her musical *Mamma Mia!* opened in London's West End in 1999 and the show was an instant success, selling out every night for weeks in advance. And that was just the start. *Mamma Mia!* has since grossed over £1.5 billion at the box office, has opened in 160 major cities round the world and has been seen by over 54 million people worldwide. In 2008 it was also made into a film starring Meryl Streep and Pierce Brosnan. The film version has become one of the highest-ever grossing films in the UK and together the success of the musical and the film have made Judy Craymer one of the richest women in the country with a personal fortune of £80 million. Yes, the numbers are truly staggering.

Of course, another way to spectacularly break the rules is to turn the very notion of running a business on its head. Once upon a time business was business and doing good was something else altogether. Not anymore. These days a growing number of far-thinking entrepreneurs are proving that it is possible to start up and run a successful venture that does not have making profits as its sole aim; they can improve people's lives at the same time. What's more, social enterprises are no longer pushed to the edges of the commercial world, they are right there in the heart of it. In fact, there are now more than 55,000 social enterprises in the UK, and the number is growing.

Take Kresse Wesling and James Henrit, who make handbags, belts and wallets out of old fire hoses being thrown out by British fire brigades. Previously the decommissioned fire hoses would have been thrown into landfill sites but now Kresse and James take them and turn them into beautiful accessories, selling them via their website, **Elvisandkresse.com**. Then they donate 50 per cent of their profits to the Fire Fighters charity. The linings for the bags and wallets are all made from recycled materials too, such as textiles from old office furniture, scrap sail cloth and waste parachute silk. The two of them also make shopping bags for the supermarket chain J Sainsbury made from old coffee sacks, which would have otherwise been thrown away.

As Kresse says: "We are firm believers that you are not going to save the planet with a doom and gloom message. You are going to save it by making it fun and exciting and engaging for everybody."

Never forget, your business can be anything you want it to be. If you think you have found a better way of doing things than conventional wisdom would suggest, then follow your instincts and do it that way. Your success will be all the sweeter.

Rachel Bridge is an author, journalist and public speaker.

WWW.RACHELBRIDGE.COM

Mentoring

by Mike Southon

"If you are making your way in business, find a mentor. If you can share the skills you've learned, become a mentor."

– Sir Richard Branson

AFTER MORE THAN 30 years as an entrepreneur, I have come to exactly the same conclusion as Richard Branson articulates in this quote. I could even go further; I am now convinced that the single most important success factor for any entrepreneur is their ability to find and then retain good mentors.

It is a great myth that all an entrepreneur needs is a great idea. In the last ten years, I must have heard thousands of business ideas; I have never ever heard a *really* bad one. In each case, I thought to myself, 'What a great idea – someone is going to be very successful doing this!' The only issue is whether the person who is pitching me the idea has what it takes.

Success in entrepreneurship depends on many factors: the ability to build a team, attracting the right customers, finding a particular niche in the early days, being adaptable when market conditions change and competition grows, and the gumption of an individual to actually start and then grow their business. But the entrepreneur's first step should always be to find a mentor, long before they write a formal business plan or invest significant time and money into their idea.

Chris West and I wrote *The Beermat Entrepreneur* back in 2001 as a reaction to the dotcom madness that had just passed. Ludicrous businesses had been launched with absurd valuations, based on flawed ideas backed by over-optimistic business plans that assumed that the tiresome task of securing real revenue was a bonus, not a prerequisite.

We proposed instead that businesses should first bootstrap themselves inexpensively and then grow organically, based on revenue generation, not lending or equity investment. Our prime example was The Instruction Set, a company I cofounded with two university friends in 1984.

I started the sales process by selling a course we had not written yet to someone who trusted us enough to pay money upfront. We then sold the company for a very tidy sum just five years later, having grown to 150 people both here and in the USA. We had no external investors, a million pounds in the bank and had been profitable for 59 of the 60 months.

Our success was due to our being in the right place at the right time and then hiring people better than ourselves, who we then allowed to do their jobs without excessive interference.

Looking back, I did not realise at the time the amount of mentoring we had all received along the way, from friends, customers and even our own staff. The measure of this is that all of these individuals have since become life-long friends; we still have regular company reunions, 20 years after the company was sold.

This ideal cycle of business was distilled into the model for entrepreneurship that Chris and I detailed in our book. We imagined a couple of friends going to a pub and writing their good ideas on a beermat. On the front cover of the book was what we called 'The Original Beermat' and on this was written three items: "Elevator Pitch; Mentor; First Customer".

The writing of a good elevator pitch is a noble art in itself. Some elevator pitches I have heard assume the lift gets stuck for several hours; others are vague to the point of abstraction – at the end of the pitch you have no concrete idea of the business idea that is being proposed.

A good elevator pitch starts with the pain or problem (or more optimistically 'opportunity') that the entrepreneur has identified. Then, there should be the premise of the business itself, described in a very literal form. Next, there should be a short description of the people involved, who are actually going to deliver the product or service, be responsible for sales and make sure the finances stack up.

At this stage the listener might be sceptical, which is why it is important to provide some proof, ideally in the form of a reference customer. Finally, the purpose of the business should be explained; of course the entrepreneur is looking to make some money, but there should be a win for the customer as well. This should not just be a good deal; a true Beermat Entrepreneur is also looking to make the world a better place.

So a good elevator pitch has five 'Ps': Pain, Premise, People, Proof and Purpose. One of the first tasks of any mentor is to work with the entrepreneur to make sure their elevator pitch actually passes muster.

Developing a good elevator pitch is a great activity for two friends in a pub or restaurant. One of them could be an extrovert, thinking about the benefits of their idea from the customer's perspective. The other might be more introverted, worrying about the quality and integrity of their proposed product or service.

Later, they can enlist the help of a third friend, someone good with spreadsheets, who can model their business and work out how to scale it for growth.

Once the elevator pitch has been prepared, Chris' and my advice was to find a mentor; someone who can provide some invaluable but free advice. The word 'free' is very important here. In our model, mentoring is always free, given with a good heart and without any ulterior motive.

It is, of course, entirely legitimate to charge for advice if you are a consultant, coach, counsellor or other professional advisor. Your opinion is valuable, and you have every right to charge for your services, so long as the commercial arrangements are clear and transparent.

But I always advise entrepreneurs to be very circumspect about free advice offered as 'mentoring' when it is merely a prequel to paid services of some kind, such as business or personal coaching.

Mentoring should always be provided by people with no current financial pressures; they have already achieved success and their business is currently trading profitably. They are mentoring because they want to, rather than have to; repaying the good fortune they have received along the way, or as the actor Kevin Spacey neatly puts it, trying "to send the elevator back down".

Since our book was released over ten years ago I have mentored over 1,000 people face-to-face. I am able to do so because I have established a successful career as a professional speaker, delivering over 100 keynote presentations and workshops every year.

This may seem like a full schedule, but it only works out as between two and three days per week, enabling me to mentor as many as six people in a single day. The mentees vary greatly, from young people brimming with several good business ideas to more experienced (and often exasperated) entrepreneurs with several years' track record wondering if and how to sell their businesses.

Over the years, I have developed a simple but effective methodology for mentoring, which I now pass onto others as often as possible. You can explain how to make money in the early days, and as success arrives, how to leave a lasting legacy.

This legacy will not just benefit your family, but also your employees and others you may never meet, perhaps people from less-privileged backgrounds who leverage your knowledge and indirectly share in your good fortune.

The key to good mentoring is self-awareness for both the mentor and mentee. I once asked a great mentor, Sir Philip Trousdell, for his advice on picking leaders, based on his many years' military experience, most notably as commandant at Sandhurst.

He explained that the British Army had been successfully using psychometric testing since the 1940s, so once I have received the mentee's one-page elevator pitch, I recommend an inexpensive third-party profiling system invented originally by my friend Roger Hamilton as Wealth Dynamics, later developed into a corporate team-building system, Talent Dynamics, by Michelle Clarke (**www.talent-dynamics.com**).

This test asks a few simple, multiple-choice questions and gives an easily understandable output report. It explains that there are eight different profiles and gives examples of entrepreneurs in each category, with the paths they took to ensure their own success.

For the mentor, this gives an invaluable analysis on the mentee's strengths and weaknesses. It also shows who might have the opposite but complementary characteristics. This represents their 'foil', the next member of the team.

Early stage entrepreneurs' first questions are usually around the question of how they are going to achieve their goals, how to deliver, sell and financially manage their chosen products and services. Typically, they approach a mentor with specific knowledge in a particular technology or market.

But even these experts do not have unlimited knowledge, so the question moves from 'how?' to 'who?', identifying and hopefully recommending someone they know who has the specific skills they lack. At this stage, the mentor should think carefully whether they really want to recommend the mentee to someone in their close network.

The most important factor is that they both like each other, enough to spend another precious hour in each other's company. If they do not relish meeting each other again, the process should not be forced, and they should both go their separate ways. But if they both enjoy each other's company, then the mentoring process is working.

One of the most important contacts that a mentor can provide is the final item on our original beermat: the first customer. Here is someone who the mentor can recommend to try out the mentee's products or services.

This should be an initial, small order, to enable the first customer to evaluate the mentee's elevator pitch. If the final deliverable does not pass muster, they can then provide invaluable feedback without taking too much of a commercial risk.

If, however, the first customer is genuinely satisfied, then this represents proof in the form of an invaluable reference and case study. The challenge is then replicating this success, building the team, and seeking out other mentors for their new challenges and opportunities.

The mentor is then able to move to the question 'why?' In the early days it is all about making a profit, the simplest measure of success of any business. But for entrepreneurs there is a very narrow margin between the confidence they need to start a business and arrogance, which can often follow success.

The prevailing impression of business is that it is all about ruthless behaviour and systematic bullying, a view promulgated by television programmes such as *Dragons' Den* and *The Apprentice*.

The reality is quite different. When I mentor university students, five out of six ideas are social enterprises, potentially profitable businesses that also have a social benefit to society. This restores my faith in humanity and optimism about the next generation of entrepreneurs and illustrates the main benefit for the mentors themselves from taking time to help the next generation of entrepreneurs.

I have experience in 17 start-ups, suffering disaster at times as well as enjoying significant success. I have learned more about entrepreneurship through mentoring than from all my experience in start-ups. The mentor always learns more in the process than the mentee, not just about business, but about themselves; as you get older, you realise you never stop learning.

The first advice I always give mentees comes from my favourite mentor, Sir Campbell Fraser, a former chairman of Scottish Television and Dunlop, who later was chairman of a start-up I was involved in.

Every morning he arrived at our office at eight o'clock and sat in the boardroom, available to anyone who wanted a chat. I used to drop in every day when I was not out on the road selling our software.

Back in 1995, he foresaw the current credit crisis, which eventually arrived 13 years later. I will never forget the advice he gave me all those years ago, delivered in his inimitable Scottish brogue: "Watch the cash laddie!"

Wise words from a wise man.

Mike Southon is a business keynote speaker, Financial Mail *columnist, entrepreneur and co-author of the best-selling* Beermat Entrepreneur *series. He can be contacted at mike@mikesouthon.com.*

WWW.MIKESOUTHON.COM

Attracting Equity Finance

by Guy Rigby

IT IS OFTEN assumed that raising external, or third party, equity is a prerequisite to business success. In the majority of cases, this could not be further from the truth.

Most businesses start with very limited funding. This is typically provided by the founder, or by family and friends on an informal basis. As these businesses develop, they bootstrap their growth, using their own profits and assets to finance their needs. As a result, they get to keep their potentially valuable equity in the hands of the founder or the family, along with the choices and freedom that brings.

Keeping it in the family is generally the preferred choice for most businesses. However, some find that cash constraints or growth opportunities make it either necessary or desirable to raise additional finance. If this cannot be found through borrowing or other non-equity sources, then raising external equity may be the only option.

If you want to attract external equity, whether from a business angle, an institutional investor or even a corporate investor, a number of boxes will need to be ticked. Here are ten of the key drivers:

1. First impressions

You only get one chance to make a first impression, so make sure you get it right. Many investors will decide not to proceed within the first 30 seconds of any discussion, or within a minute or two of picking up your business plan. Here's how you can make sure you give it your best shot:

- Understand who you are talking to by doing detailed research in advance. Where it is available, review your target investor's criteria carefully to ensure that you and your business will fit. Don't try to put a square peg in a round hole.

- Dress sensibly, be on time, know your market and understand your shortcomings. Think about your approach, test it on your friends and practise it to perfection. Don't fall at the first fence.

- Explain clearly and concisely what you do and what you are trying to achieve. Build a picture of the future in your investor's mind. Avoid the use of hearsay and jargon. Stick to the facts and keep it simple.

- Be enthusiastic, but realistic. Don't make outrageous claims or forecasts. Investors may get close to accepting the impossible, but miracles are definitely a stretch.

2. Vision and strategy

Your investor will want to understand your vision and your business strategy.

You will need to demonstrate your competitive advantage in your chosen area and explain why your particular approach will succeed. Have you got some IP that will disrupt the existing market? Have you got a newer, better, faster or cheaper business model? Or do you simply have a profitable existing business that requires funding for local or international expansion?

"VCs are not gamblers, they're astute business people," says Seb Bishop, founder of Espotting. "They like to invest in a proven model."

Investors have to be able to buy-in to the overall vision. This requires the communication of that vision in an articulate and appealing way.

"In my experience," says Julie Meyer, co-founder of First Tuesday, Ariadne Capital and the Entrepreneur Country movement, "the better the entrepreneur is at articulating the core vision and developing the brand early, the easier and better the financing has been."

Taking that 'elevator pitch' methodology to the extreme, investor Simon Dolan requested pitches through Twitter saying that the discipline of pitching within the 140 character limit helps to "focus the mind".

Similarly, Bill Morrow, founder of Angels Den, has pioneered the practice of 'speed funding'. "We have thousands of companies registered and some of them are brilliant, yet they are unlikely to get funded via speed funding because they cannot explain easily, quickly and concisely what it is that the company does," says Bill. "Some people say, 'three minutes? That's far too short.' And yet three minutes is more than enough time to hang yourself."

3. Business plan

A well-thought-out and comprehensive business plan is an essential part of any investment proposition. Make sure yours includes detailed and plausible information on where you see the business in three to five years, along with the clearly identified critical success factors that you'll achieve along the way.

4. Management team

Your pitch should clearly demonstrate the capabilities and competencies of your team, giving assurance to your investor that they have the skills and experience to manage the business and maximise its potential. Be aware that the skills and experience required to run a smaller business may differ from those required by a larger business. If any skills are missing it may be worth bringing someone in or identifying a prospective candidate with a suitable skill set prior to seeking investment.

Brian Livingston, head of mergers and acquisitions at Smith & Williamson, spent 13 years at private equity house, 3i. "When considering investing in a business, we used three criteria: management, management and management," says Brian, who adds that it's not about having the best product, but more about being in the best market with the best team behind that product.

"In a perfect world you are looking for a good management team in a good sector that is cash-generative, with a well-thought-out business plan and an established market position. Or, as someone once said to me, 'You always want to back a digger but, ideally, they should be digging on top of a gold mine.' The continuum is that you could have a good team digging in a bad sector or a bad team digging in a good sector. The latter can do OK for a while, and a good team digging in a bad sector can do better than anybody else, but not very well. So what you really need is a good team in a good sector. It's that winning combination," concludes Brian.

Investor James Caan's advice echoes the importance placed on the management team when evaluating investment opportunities. "Management quality is the single most important intangible that outweighs all others when assessing the future potential of any business," says James. "What the business will do in the future relies very much on how the management thinks, how they operate and how they make business decisions."

To evaluate the quality of the management, James looks at the team's growth aspirations and plans, its financial track record and how it has grown the business since it was founded. He also considers whether it has delivered on 'bringing business in' and whether its overall understanding of the business "demonstrates how well the team is in control".

"A combination of functional, operational and well-rounded business expertise would command premium value," adds James, who also assesses the ability of a company "to attract, motivate, incentivise and retain talent at all levels."

"This is another key intangible that drives value," comments James. "If the management has set up a business that is attracting and retaining talent then the future value of the business is more assured."

For this reason, James, who famously backs people rather than their ideas, examines the incentive structure in a business to see how aligned it is with its growth aspirations, as this has an impact on efficiency and productivity. He also evaluates the operational infrastructure and mindset, seeking well-structured training programmes and an underlying mentality of excellence as a driving force.

5. Trust and transparency

Investors don't like surprises – they demand honesty and transparency. The quickest way to lose a potential investor is to sacrifice trust by embellishing the truth. Integrity is the name of the game and no business is ever entirely problem free.

"Nobody expects everything to be completely and utterly perfect," says Brad Rosser. "So treat investors with common sense; be honest about the entire business from day one. Anything other than the truth slows deals down or kills them entirely."

Honesty engenders trust and, as Julie Meyer and Anita Roddick, founder of The Body Shop, have both said, "Trust is efficient."

In general, investment doesn't happen until 'due diligence' has been completed. Due diligence is a process of discovery normally carried out by professionals, designed to provide assurance to an investor in relation to the current state of affairs of the business, as well as its future prospects. If there are false claims or misstatements, they are likely to be discovered at this due diligence stage, often resulting in the withdrawal of the prospective investor. Even if they escape detection through due diligence, the problems are likely to surface later on, damaging the relationship with your new investor and potentially undermining your future.

So don't bury bad news or focus only on the positives – just tell it like it is. If there are problems in particular areas, highlight them and explain how you will address them. By doing this, you will gain the trust and support of your investor, who will probably offer to help.

6. Advisors

They say that you're only as good as the company you keep and as Henry Kissinger, the American politician and Nobel Peace Prize laureate, famously said, "Ninety per cent of the politicians give the other ten per cent a bad reputation."

Raising external equity can involve a bevy of advisors, including accountants and lawyers on both sides and, often, a number of other experts. It's important that you select experienced advisors who are both appropriate to the size of the transaction and who have seen it and done it before.

Brian Livingston comments: "It's a question of horses for courses. You don't appoint the largest law firm to the smallest deal or vice versa, but you should always use someone who is known at the appropriate level in the market, and who the investor's advisors respect."

Getting the right advice when you take in new investment can be crucial to your future wealth. There will almost certainly be an agreement containing clauses designed to protect the investor and you will need to understand these and work with your advisor to negotiate the best possible outcome.

Many entrepreneurs are in too much of a hurry at this stage, with the challenge and buzz of raising the funding giving way to the less interesting aspects of completing investment agreements and other formalities. Don't be one of the many who only discover what they have signed up to after it's too late.

So choose your advisors carefully and let them have the difficult conversations. Listen to their advice and use them as your gladiator to help you achieve your goals.

As Brian Livingston says: "I call it the Goldilocks Principle – businesses should use advisors who are not too hot and not too cold, but just right."

7. Financial results and forecasts

It goes without saying that your business plan will include your historic financial statements as well as realistic assumptions and forecasts supporting your future trading activity.

Be particularly prepared for questions around your working capital, the engine of your ongoing solvency, and consider the effectiveness of your KPIs and regular management information. Don't just leave an understanding of this crucial area to your finance director or your financial advisors. This will probably not be enough to reassure your investor of your financial acumen and your ability to manage and grow his investment.

So take time out with your finance director or your financial advisors so that you fully understand your numbers and the drivers affecting your cash flow and profitability. Become familiar with commonly used financial language and its meaning. Finally, be aware of key threats and sensitivities.

8. Funding requirement and purpose

Your financial forecasts will incorporate the funding you are seeking, although it may be difficult to forecast the precise financial impact. This is because the investment you receive may ultimately be structured so that only part of the funding is reflected as equity, with the balance being treated as preferred capital or as a loan. Until the eventual funding structure is known, it will be impossible to finalise your forecasts.

Notwithstanding this, your business plan should include a separate section setting out the amount you are seeking and the purpose for which it is sought. In this way, your investor will be able to identify precisely what it is that he is funding and will be able to weigh up the likely consequences of his investment.

It is often difficult to assess exactly how much funding you will need. Whilst you will obviously allow for contingencies, your investor will be keen to ensure that you are not cutting it too fine. Think long term, as he would far rather provide additional funding at the outset than find a shortfall emerging later on.

9. Valuation and pricing

There are a number of ways of valuing a business. These will vary dependent upon the type of business, its profitability, its maturity and its future prospects. In a start-up, values are often extremely difficult to assess, whereas this can be easier in more mature businesses.

Work with your advisors to establish a sensible valuation for your business. Whether this is based on hope value, assets or earnings, don't be tempted to overvalue your ideas or achievements. We are a long way from the heady dotcom days when investors were persuaded to part with large amounts of cash based on little more than an idea. Nothing will put an investor off more quickly than an excessive or insupportable valuation.

Remember that external equity can be expensive. The more you need, the more you will have to give away, so be realistic, cut your cloth and take in as little external funding as possible.

10. Exit

It's very easy for an investor to put money into your business, but how will he get it back? A vague idea that you would like to buy his shares back at some future date is unlikely to be attractive. Taking in external equity means that you often need to 'begin at the end' in terms of thinking about exit, having a clear strategy and plan.

Who are the likely buyers of your business? What will the business need to look like in order to be attractive to them? Will the sale be to a trade buyer or competitor or might the business be attractive to a financial investor, such as a private equity firm? If the current funding round is the first step on the road to a buy-and-build strategy, where will the next round of funding come from? Should you be considering an IPO for the business?

These are yet more issues to discuss with your advisors. Plans may change as the business grows, but be aware of the possibilities and put your initial stake in the ground.

Guy Rigby is Head of the Entrepreneurial Services Group at Smith & Williamson.

To discuss attracting equity finance for your business in more detail, contact Guy Rigby on 020 7131 8213, or email guy.rigby@smith.williamson.co.uk.

WWW.GUYRIGBY.COM

The Future of Raising Finance

by Simon Dixon

IT IS EASY to think that raising finance for your business will be hard when banks are not lending, people seem to have less money to invest and the economy gets worse.

However, nothing could be further from the truth. There are very generous tax breaks for people who invest in businesses like yours; there is more money out there for investing than ever before; and there is a completely new type of investor waiting to invest in you.

You do need to be looking in the right places to get it, though.

If your strategy for raising finance is scattershot, you will experience a lot of rejection, frustration and most importantly … waste a lot of your valuable time. It is tragic, but many people never get their product and business launched, simply because they waste time pitching for the wrong source of finance.

If only they knew that there are willing investors for different types of businesses and projects, but they all hang out in different places and speak different languages.

Beware of making the same mistake!

If you wanted to raise finance for your business or project in the past, you either had rich friends and family members, a great network of high net worth individuals, a high-growth business getting you referrals to venture capitalists (VCs), were launching in a bubble and could raise finance on a stock market for just an idea, or managed to persuade a bank manager who knew nothing about business that you had a good business!

Well, the landscape has changed a lot.

A whole new world

Everything has changed in two big ways – and there is good news and bad news. The good news: new sources of money have opened up for you. The bad news: old sources of finance have closed.

So let's get the bad news out of the way.

As a business, entrepreneur or somebody looking to raise finance for your project, banks do not want to play with you anymore. Full stop. Simply put, banks have choices when they make a loan. They can lend money to somebody who has a nice secure job and gets paid every month from a large company. They can lend it to somebody taking out a mortgage and if everything goes wrong the bank will still get the house. Or … they can lend it to your business, which has limited liability if it all goes wrong.

If you are involved in a business with unpredictable cash flows, what will make a bank pick you?

Exactly. So banks are out of the market. In fact, in the future I don't think they will want to play with small businesses or project finance at all. Leave the banks to credit cards and mortgages; they don't want to help you.

Who does? Well, not VCs either – not right away, anyway. Today, in the UK, there is no real VC market. At least, they don't want to invest in new ventures; they only want to invest once you have proven you can grow big.

In other words, there's not much point looking at VCs until you have proven that your business is strapped to a rocket in a high growth market.

Which brings us back to the good news. There are plenty of new sources of money in town to help you get there. They break down into three main categories.

Crowd funding

Here's how crowd funding works:

You upload a pitch to a crowd-funding website, detailing how you are going to create your product, and you offer non-monetary rewards in return for people (the crowd) investing. For example, you could offer a copy of your product once it is complete to those who contribute £10, a VIP launch party invite to those who contribute £100, and so on.

You then promote this until your funding goal is met or its deadline passes. If your funding goal is met, you get the money and have to deliver upon your promises. If not, you get nothing and the money is returned.

This type of finance is most appropriate for those seeking money for a specific product or those at the idea stage and fairly early start-up.

The money does not need to be repaid and it does not cost you any equity!

Crowd lending

Crowd lending lets you borrow money for your business from a crowd of private lenders. After applying you are credit-assessed and passed through a risk model. If you meet the criteria for a good risk, then you are matched up with hundreds of lenders who all want to lend you money for an agreed monthly repayment, interest and duration.

The crowd-lending platform manages all repayments once you receive the money. Because there is no bank to pay, both parties get a better rate on their money.

At **BankToTheFuture.com** we call these BankToTheFuture (BF) CrowdLoans.

This type of finance is most appropriate for businesses with good cash flow, a good credit rating and trading history.

Crowd investing

Just like a public company offers shares to the public, a crowd investment allows you to offer shares in your private company to the crowd online, for a desired level of equity at a valuation you set.

Instead of rewards, the crowd become shareholders. If you successfully meet your funding goal, the platform helps you manage investor relations once completed.

Investors invest in high-risk prospects for the opportunity of dividends and a lucrative exit, just like an angel or a VC.

The big difference is that it brings in new sources of money much earlier; as it is not restricted to just high-net-worth angels, it opens up investment opportunities for ordinary people and fans, suppliers, customers, joint venture partners and so on.

We call these BankToTheFuture (BF) CrowdInvestments.

This is the most appropriate option for investment-ready businesses that can pitch a good business case for investors.

And you?

The different types of crowd finance can be useful at different times in your business journey. You might find yourself using them all, just at different stages.

- Starting from scratch, you could raise finance for your idea without giving away equity or having to repay the loan through a crowd fund.

- If you deliver upon your promise and make progress, you could then raise further finance through a crowd investment by offering shares to the crowd.

- As the business progresses you could apply for a crowd loan, allowing you to get yourself ready for a VC if you want to scale the business as you are experiencing high growth.

This then opens up more traditional private equity, banks and capital markets as you grow.

A new model of finance

So in summary, we are moving towards a new model of finance:

- banks will serve personal debt and mortgages

- crowd funds and crowd investments will serve early-stage projects and businesses

- angels will more frequently start managing their early-stage investments through crowd investing platforms, as the crowd investment market gets more sophisticated

- crowd loans will serve businesses seeking loans for working capital, development and growth

- VCs will serve businesses that need to scale fast in a growing market

- banks, capital markets and private equity houses will still be used for large companies.

So there you have it. Don't waste your time with the wrong source of finance. Spend your time getting investment ready for the right source of finance – and that's the source that is right for you.

Getting investment ready

Once you know the correct source of finance, you need to get yourself investment ready.

Avoid making the mistake of sending a business plan written for a bank to a busy angel investor …

… or creating a video pitch laying out the business case for a crowd investment, when you should have created a viral video with crowd funding in mind …

… or even worse, not having your slide deck ready after speaking to an interested investor. Get this wrong, and you will fail in the first contact with investors.

There are seven potential documents that you will need to have ready before you approach a funding round. Depending on what type of money you are seeking, you will need different documents before you start approaching investors.

First things first. Start with a business plan.

1. Business plan

Avoid making the mistake of using one of the many free business plan templates that you find online that has been written with a bank in mind and covers over 80 pages.

Your business plan needs to be written for the reader. If you are approaching a bank, then these templates will work. But banks are way more interested in the financial model than anything else.

A business plan for a non-bank is meant to be a marketing document, not a boring business plan template.

Investors care about two things – return on investment and risk.

These need to be addressed in your marketing plan, your management team description, your executive summary, your market summary, your financial plan and all the other sections of your business plan.

The reason we start with the business plan is because it is the most comprehensive document. It can be used to produce the other documents that are important for raising finance.

2. Financial plan

The financial plan needs to paint the picture that is described in the business plan. It is the numerical version of the story.

Remember, if it is written for a VC, there is no point in having a financial model that ends in a £1m revenue business! They will throw it in the bin as it is too small. On the other hand, if that is the truth, don't lie, just stop approaching VCs and look at other sources.

If you are seeking finance through a crowd investment, remember to construct the financial model so it can be easily understood as a standalone document. Make a quick summary of the key figures for your slide deck too. You will need a cash flow forecast, a balance sheet and a profit and loss account for a minimum of three years, and a maximum of five. Beware of making up your own jargon. Use the normal accounting standards so it isn't hard for sophisticated investors who are used to reading forecasts.

If you are raising finance through a crowd fund, don't waste your time on preparing this for public consumption, but do make sure the numbers add up and you'll be able to satisfy your funders at the end of it all. They just won't want to see it in your pitch; they care more about your video and story.

For a crowd loan, the financial plan is the most important document.

3. Slide deck

The slide deck is where you take the business plan and condense it down into ten to 15 slides full of beautiful visuals, catchy sentences, and relevant information that addresses the key things that investors care about:

- a clear elevator pitch

- the problem you are solving

- your solution to the problem

- the size of your market

- your business model

- your product/technology

- your competition

- your marketing plan

- your team

- and your financials.

Keep it brief and complete. A real challenge, I know, but this is the one document that busy people will look at. It is essential for crowd investments and pitches to angels and VCs, but less important to banks, and irrelevant to crowd funds.

If you are seeking crowd funding and crowd investment finance, the next one is your main focus …

4. Video pitch

If you are raising finance through a crowd fund or crowd investment, by far the most important part of your pitch is your video.

You need to give people something worth sharing that is easy to watch. Most people don't have time to download and read documents, but many more will make time for a compelling video.

The most important part of your video pitch is the first 8–16 seconds. Sixty per cent of investors will decide whether they want to continue watching your video pitch in the first few seconds. You need to hook them in quickly.

After hooking them in, you need to give your story in less than a minute, followed by your video pitch. If it is for a crowd investment, your pitch needs to walk them through the business case. If it is for a crowd fund, give some kind of demonstration of your product, prototype, movie, whatever it is you are seeking finance for.

Just make sure you include your story: the emotion is what people commit to.

When crowd funding, avoid being boring and stiff. When crowd investing, remember to lay out the business case. In the latter case you will need to be aware of compliance issues, too; you don't want to promise any kind of returns, just stick to what you want to do and what you are doing now.

You can go simple with a video using your smartphone, or go all out with a professional production. The more thought you put into the video, the more money you can raise.

5. Half-page summary

Have a short and easy to read half-page summary of the opportunity your business presents, and keep it ready to copy and paste.

Some call it an executive summary, but make it even shorter that. And eliminate all jargon. Write it in simple English so everybody can understand it.

You will need this when writing emails, and when submitting your business or project for crowd funds, crowd investments and crowd loans. So have it ready. Take the key points from your slide deck and get it down to a brief summary that anybody can quickly read in an email.

6. Tax

It is unforgivable to not structure your investment in a way that is tax beneficial for your investors. Make sure you have done your research, because your competition for investment will.

Obviously, if you are crowd funding, it does not matter. But for crowd investments and offering equity to investors, there are tax schemes in the UK that can make you a lot cheaper to investors than your competition.

For example, if you were incorporated within the last two years and are raising up to £150,000 through a crowd investment, you might qualify for SEIS, which to the right investor gets them a 78% kick-back on their investment, making an investment of £100,000 in you only a £22,000 risk.

This can, obviously, make a big difference in how likely people are to invest in you.

7. Legals

You will need articles of association that lay out the terms of your deal if you are seeking equity finance through a crowd investment. Are you offering voting rights? Dividend rights? A shares? B shares? Pre-emption? Drag along? Tag along? Etc., etc.

A good crowd investing, crowd funding and crowd lending platform should be able to give you the right level of protection and help to get the right legal documents you will need in this process and to save you a lot of the cost.

If you are seeking finance through a crowd fund, you will need to deliver upon the rewards you offer. So don't promise anything you cannot deliver.

VCs will want way more from you in their term sheet than any other type of investor, so you will need to consider the consequences. If it all goes wrong, you can end up being ousted from your own company!

Simon Dixon is CEO of BankToTheFuture.

BANKTOTHEFUTURE.COM

Google Me!

by Nick James

Customers do it, suppliers do it
Even your investors do it
You do it – we all do it

(With apologies to Cole Porter)

THAT'S GOOGLING PEOPLE rather than falling in love, but in today's ever connected and 'always on' world it might just be as dangerous a game to ignore your online footprint as to marry in haste.

I have worked with a number of clients who have almost left it too late to create and then curate their online presence. One of them was even refused a visa as a result of such limited information being available that only an inaccurate and decades-old news story could be found.

Today's search engines return information at the click of a mouse but the search engine results pages (SERPS) can only display the information that is available to them about you or your business.

Google and the other major search engines rely on an algorithm to hunt out and archive information on the world wide web and you have a certain amount of control over that information. PR companies that run crisis media training rightly say that if you wait for the crisis to happen with no plan in place then it's often too late; the same is true of your digital footprint.

There used to be a saying, "Never pick a fight with someone who buys their ink by the barrel", referring to the press barons of old; in today's world, if you have a strong social media presence at least you have a platform that gives you the ability to reply – but where to start and what to do?

SEO your CEO

If the CEO is you then you must take some responsibility, even if it means delegating the job to someone else. You need a communications plan.

There are some things that are must-dos.

LinkedIn

LinkedIn is easy to use and allows you to create a network of people that you can quickly communicate with as well as providing you with an easy way of sharing information and even positioning yourself as a thought leader.

An individual's LinkedIn profile will be logged and archived by Google and often features at the top of the SERPS when searching for somebody and their business. Unless you're a personal super brand such as Richard Branson with hundreds of websites profiling you, it's likely that your LinkedIn profile will feature at the top of the Google results – and you have complete control over what it says.

Your LinkedIn profile is too important to ignore. Sparse information or few connections in the industry you work in can suggest that you're not connected and therefore not really important!

Wikipedia

Wikipedia is another profile that you should pay attention to. You don't have anything like the control over it as you do over LinkedIn, but you can identify and report inaccuracies.

Twitter

The tour de force that is Twitter deserves a chapter of its own, but suffice to say that now that traditional media search the micro-blogging site to quote people on just about every topic, Twitter is most definitely mainstream.

I'm **@freshnick** on Twitter and by no means an expert or guru but I spend about 30 minutes a day reading and posting – as a reformed smoker, it's my cigarette break that not only allows me to keep up to date with news and views but also gives me a communications channel that is fuelled by the crowd.

I've used it to complain on occasion and the results were close to immediate. I've also arranged ad hoc business meetings in airport lounges, been retweeted (RT'd) by sector experts and even got into an argument with Piers Morgan.

It's often been said that Twitter is like a conversation in the pub, and it is. Like a conversation in the pub it needs to be two-way; you need to turn the knob to receive as well as transmit, it's not a broadcast medium and authenticity is the name of the game.

Google will serve up your Twitter profile in its search results as it will for any profile you have on its own social network Google+. I can hear the groans of people thinking that they don't have the time or inclination to spend hours telling the world at large that they're popping out for a coffee but it doesn't need to be that banal. You can use it for information, news, ideas, advice and even inspiration while at the same time adding substance to your own reputation.

Compelling content

The phrase 'everyone's a publisher now' is absolutely true. Never before have we mere mortals had the ability to communicate directly with an audience with such immediacy and Twitter, LinkedIn and Facebook are in many ways the delivery and amplification channels.

But if you really want to make an indelible digital mark then you should start blogging and then use social media to point people in the direction of your pearls of wisdom. Your blog can either be a standalone publication where you are writer, editor, publisher and paperboy (pushing your journal through email or social media letterboxes) or you can approach relevant industry and business publications or even trade associations who in most cases will be only too pleased to have regular and relevant fresh content.

Our own online magazines, including **www.freshbusinessthinking. com**, rely on regular contributions from experts, commentators and thought leaders and as we have a modicum of 'status', postings from contributors find their way to the top of the SERPS.

Once you have published a post you are then able to amplify using your social weapon of choice and with a bit of luck you will get some 'internet love' and people will linkback it.

Link love

Getting linkbacks is really important, as links are the online equivalent of a vote of approval and as such carry a massive amount of weight when it comes to being found online. Google's algorithm relies heavily on links. The more authoritative the person or organisation that links to you, the more weight that link carries.

PageRank, named after Google founder Larry Page, is largely link-based and recent algorithm updates (in particular Panda and Penguin) are rewarding sites that generate good links as much as they are penalising bad links (paid-for or obviously fabricated). As a result of this, most online publications will welcome genuine contributions from individuals with something to say.

If you employ a PR agency or have someone in-house, get them to approach the leading publications in your industry. Alternatively, if your business is regional or local get in touch with the local or regional media. Let them know that you're happy to provide comment or write full posts; you will be surprised at their willingness to work with you.

Video

The importance of video in SEO is not a complete surprise considering that Google owns YouTube. Search engines like video content – especially if it's interesting and relevant. Creating quality video is now affordable for even the smallest of business; and now that most people have access to fast broadband, it is easy to access.

Nowadays a video blog doesn't have to have the high production values it did a few years ago. Like any communication it mostly needs to be thought through, relevant and contextual and needs to add value to a target audience.

But that target audience can now be niche; so think narrowcasting rather than broadcasting. Video on YouTube and other platforms can be shared, linked to and found via search engines in exactly the same way as with 'plain text' or images. Targeting your audience really precisely will help with that.

Conclusion

Whether you like it or not, you and your business have an online reputation that may or may not be positive, and if you're proactive you have more control over it. At worst you can identify and respond to bad reviews, comments or negativity, at best you can be recognised as a thought leader and expert.

So, if you are ever confronted with a crisis, those of you who are proactive when it comes to your online presence will be better equipped to deal with it, will be better informed about you industry and sector and in addition might even meet some interesting people.

> *Employees I might add do it*
> *Your local bank manager might even do it*
> *Most definitely your kids will do it*
> *Let's do it, let's fall in love (with Google)*

Nick James is founder of Fresh Business Thinking.

WWW.FRESHBUSINESSTHINKING.COM

Hiring a PR Agency
by Anne Cantelo

G OOD PR CAN can change your position in the marketplace and give you authority and credibility – qualities that are usually a struggle to achieve for a young business.

However, PR can take time to deliver tangible results and, in some markets, it is unlikely to ever deliver the return on investment you need. So what is PR and when is it worth spending your valuable time and start-up budget on it? How can you be sure you get a return for your investment?

You need to ask whether PR is right for you when writing your marketing plan and asking all the usual marketing questions – clarifying the audience you want to engage, the customer journey, the competition and your budget. Most brands find that they need a combination of marketing tools, but focus their budget and time on some tools more than others. The main reason PR is included in the marketing mix is because people believe third-party endorsement far more than self-promotion, and they believe their friends most of all (hence the effectiveness of social media). So PR – which means inspiring, persuading or encouraging *others* to share your marketing messages – can be the most powerful marketing tool of all.

In many markets PR can also be one of the cheapest ways to reach new audiences. However, PR for some products and services can be tough and demand more investment to see any impact: if it is difficult to explain your product and your market is very niche, the PR opportunities are likely to be more limited. It is also sometimes not immediately obvious what the returns are from PR; there can be a weak immediate link between sales and coverage. You can track the audience you're reaching but converting them into customers may take time.

Once you've decided you should invest in PR, you need to consider whether you can and should fulfil the role in-house. The advantage of doing PR in-house is that an employee will know your business and should see what is going on better than an outsider, without you having to spend a lot of time briefing. They may also pick up on sensitivities and when you're under pressure and unable to give time to PR. Contrary to popular perception, though, for a small company this is not usually the cheaper option. Many of the essential software tools that PR agencies use to reach journalists and track what they're writing about are very expensive. That cost, in an agency, is spread across many clients.

Do you understand how PR works and how it differs from advertising? Do you have the skills to manage PR in-house? At its most simplistic, PR is getting other people to say positive things about you. Getting other people to mention you, whether in print or online, requires careful consideration of the needs of that third party.

What makes a good story that will interest a journalist? All stories will have at least one of the following elements, and often more than one:

1. **Scandal:** Contrary to popular myth, not all publicity is good publicity. PR makes you more visible and some people may

want to shoot you down, so you need to look carefully at your 'dirty washing'. What is the worst that someone could say about you? For example, don't set yourself up as a family-friendly company if you have just sacked a pregnant employee. You may have had good reasons for the dismissal and would win in court, but it is easier and cheaper to highlight something else to avoid the possible backlash. People don't always remember the outcome of a story, just the mud that was originally slung. The media's love of scandal can, if carefully handled, be used to your advantage. But companies should use this approach with great caution.

2. **Topical:** You should have a good knowledge of what the media are talking about so that you can relate your story to it. Sometimes this is stretched too far. A journalist friend of mine got a press release linking spatulas to Valentine's Day. If the media are all talking about a subject that is relevant to you then you may have a chance of adding your voice (if you're *very* quick).

3. **Original:** News has to be new. Most respected journalists (as opposed to content creators) will not write about something that is already in the public domain unless it moves the story on. So if you announce your wonderful new product on social media, don't expect a journalist to want to write about it a week later. It's old news. The media engage us by telling us things that are out of the ordinary. How far are you willing to go? Richard Branson crossed the Atlantic in numerous different vehicles and wore make-up for one launch to make his story stand out.

4. **Relevant:** The media are very specific about their target audience. Each of the women's magazines, for example, knows the exact age range of their readers and will not take case studies that are either older or younger (or from men).

However, do remember that hairdressers are more likely to read the *Sun* than *Hairdressers Journal*. And did you read the *Metro* this morning or *Start Your Business*?

5. **Human interest:** People are interested in people. That's why the media love case studies that illustrate the story and show how someone's life has been improved by a product or service, so try to put a human element into your story. What difference does it make to people?

The media love infographics and good photos (particularly business media, who are often starved of good images and will include a story with very weak news value if the image is good). Looking at my copy of the *Metro* today there is a large photo of two young women smeared in 'dirt' captioned: "The only female sewage apprentices". Hardly an earth-shattering story, but the photo is good. You may also remember the image of a minor female celebrity on the top of huge Christmas tree, which was printed in all the newspapers and publicised the opening of a shopping centre to great effect.

If you go for an agency, how do you choose the right one? You will need to trust them with the reputation of your brand so it's important that you give this very careful consideration. It's not necessary to instigate a large competitive pitch, which usually wastes a lot of everyone's time. Instead, ask for personal recommendations and start by having a fairly informal chat with each of the agencies. When you meet the agencies you should consider:

1. **Do you like them as people?** You will be working closely with them so it's important that you get on.

2. **Do they care about your business?** You need a team that is passionate about your business.

3. **Do they understand your business?** They need to be able to identify the right news hooks and answer detailed questions on your behalf. Of course, they will need lots of briefing from you at the start of the relationship, but if they show a lot of ignorance when you meet them, the time you spend briefing is likely to be irritatingly protracted.

4. **Can they write?** PR is about creating stories about your brand. If they're not good writers your message will get confused (or be too boring for the media to pick up) and you'll spend hours having to correct their copy. Look for an agency with professional writers on the team.

5. **Are they specialists or generalists?** Specialists will have great relationships with the right journalists and will be quick to understand what you do. However, they're likely to have very similar companies on their books already, with a potential conflict of interest. A generalist will probably struggle with some of your jargon to start with (but that will force you to simplify) and may take slightly longer to get the results as they will need to form relationships with new journalists. However, they will then be pushing you forward for any relevant opportunity.

6. **Do they have creative ideas that will work within the constraints you have?**

Once you've hired a PR agency your job is not over. PR is not something that you can simply delegate to someone and walk away. It will take significant amounts of your time, particularly in the early days. One of my more experienced clients once said to me that a PR agency is only as good as their clients allow them to be and I've found that to be very true. I've had clients with very similar stories and the same budget and who have devoted just as much time and effort as each other. Yet one would be swamped with coverage and delighted, the other complaining that we achieved little for them.

How can you ensure you get the results you need?

1. **Be a great spokesperson.** The media use the spokespeople they do because the editors know they can rely on them to be available and talk with authority (they're not necessarily the best informed). It is well worth investing in media training.

2. **Allow the agency time to do their job.** In a small team it's tempting to get your agency to fill lots of different roles. We're happy to do that; we like to support you as a part of your team. But do remember that you pay us by the hour (we have to keep time sheets). If you use up your budget getting support for things not connected to PR then don't judge the agency on the amount of coverage they've achieved.

3. **Respond quickly to emails and phone calls from the agency.** The quicker you respond, the better the chance you have of being used in reactive opportunities.

4. **Ensure your approval process is short and quick.** The news moves on very quickly. If it takes days or even weeks to approve even a simple press release, article or comment, your coverage will be severely restricted.

5. **Trust the agency.** Everyone thinks they understand PR and everyone thinks they can write. PR professionals spend every day talking to journalists and finding out what works and what doesn't work. The arguments they're having with you now, they've had many times before. When they advise you it's therefore worth listening to them.

6. **Recognise that you have to make compromises to get the media to talk about you.** Your advertising copy simply won't work.

7. **Ensure you keep the agency well briefed and give them all the assets they need, such as professional images.** Tell them your news before it happens.

If you decide that you want to hire a PR agency, how much will it cost? Like most business services PR agencies work out how much to charge based on the time needed to deliver results. PR is a time-intensive business so the retainer fees reflect this. If you consider how much it would cost to employ someone skilled to do the work (not just the salary but all the other costs), employing an agency is not expensive. Many entrepreneurs try to do deals with PR agencies to exchange time for profit share. Please don't be offended if we turn you down, or think we doubt that your business will succeed. We have to pay our overheads at the end of the month and we're not in a position to carry the risk.

Great PR requires hard work and commitment from both you and the agency but PR can deliver astonishing results and make you look and feel absolutely fabulous!

Anne Cantelo is MD of Soho Square PR agency, Onyx,
and a writer.

ONYX-PR.COM

How to Run a Successful Business

by Christian Nellemann

A T XLN THE question 'How can we help your business?' is the core driver behind all we do. When I began selling telecoms back in 2002, it was because small business owners told me that they were paying too much to make phone calls. I realised if I could get enough small businesses together, I could offer them a better deal – and so XLN was born.

Over the years, I have learnt that to run a successful business it's crucial to have some solid foundations in place.

There are four key areas that I spend the lion's share of my time and focus on when building a new business: making sure I know my business better than anyone else, paying close attention to my business costs, effectively promoting what I am selling and making sure I hire the right people who share my vision.

Starting a business is the easy part; it's keeping it running which is tough. I hope these tips help to build your business into a success!

Part 1: How to sell

Like most people, when I was setting up in business for myself, one of the biggest challenges I faced was how to sell. Although I was convinced of the value of my products, how could I communicate that value to other people effectively?

After many years working hard at refining our sales techniques, I reckon there are four simple tricks that any business can use to make sure they are selling as much as they can, to as many people as they can.

1. Know your market

It is impossible to describe how important knowing your target market is. Yet time and again I meet would-be entrepreneurs with only a very vague sense of who would part with their hard-earned cash to buy their product or service. Are you setting up a hairdresser's shop? If so, think about your expected customers. Do they live locally? Are they likely to walk past your shop, or will they be in the car? How many people pass the front of the shop on any given day? Are your customers single, or married with children? How much money do your potential customers have available to buy your product? As I have increasingly discovered the value of knowing my customers, so it has become easier to target them.

2. Know your product

It's all very well having a target market in mind, but what are you going to sell to them? What essential need or desire are you going to help with? The fact that you've already got a business or are thinking of setting one up suggests that you already have an opportunity available. One of the best things we ever did was to adjust our product to focus more closely on the market we had chosen. It was no longer a case of selling a generic product to one particular set of people, but rather selling a tailored, suitable product to a market ready to receive it.

3. Practise your pitch

Once you have a good idea of who your target customer is and you know what you're selling, I've found there is nothing better than getting out and starting to sell! I remember when I first began selling telephone lines to the shops around Vauxhall, every day was an experiment in how best to show business owners how we could help them save money. They say practice makes perfect, and we learned a lot in those early days about what our customers saw as the most attractive features of our product and how we could get those across to them as effectively as possible.

4. Continue to refine what you do

In fact, actually talking to customers about your product helps you further refine your market and whether you need to make any changes to what you offer. The more we speak to our customers, the more we see where we can help them. At XLN we have a very efficient feedback loop where the conversations we have with customers are quickly fed back into our pricing, features and even our whole product set.

Part 2: How to buy

I've always found the fun side of setting up and running your own business is identifying something people want and then persuading them that your solution is the best one for them. But every business has another side to it, which is equally important in deciding how profitable your enterprise will be – costs. Even if you're selling the right stuff and selling lots of it, if your business costs are too high then you're not going to make money. So I reckon that paying close attention to your business costs is as critical to your success as the fun bit.

1. Squeeze your product suppliers … then squeeze them again

If you sell products then whoever sells them to you is one of your core business relationships. You may feel close to them, go to their parties and read their newsletters. But never forget they are trying to make money too and your suppliers will no doubt try to increase their prices over the years as their customer base grows and matures. Perhaps you could get cheaper prices if you looked around? Even if you rate your current suppliers highly or if they are particularly convenient, it isn't disloyal to take a look at alternatives. If you find cheaper prices elsewhere you could use them to negotiate a discount with your current provider.

2. Professional services prices vary wildly

Have you been with the same accountant for years? It can be hard to switch when they are like an old friend and know your business inside out. But there can be a big difference in the costs charged by accountants, solicitors and other professionals and it is well worth finding out the cheapest rates currently available.

3. Look hard at recurring expenses

Often we pay a lot of attention to money spent on big ticket items like shop fitting or IT equipment. But we spend less time on the small recurring costs which drain our bank accounts every month. But with only a little effort some of these might save wads of cash if they could all be trimmed. Business phone lines and broadband costs are a classic – most businesses have been with BT for years but could save 20 or 30% by switching to a cheaper supplier like XLN.

4. Property costs

Property costs like rent, mortgages, leases, etc. are really important to keep an eye on. And although you'll often have relatively lengthy contracts in place, once these are up for renewal these may be flexible, particularly if you are able to relocate your business to new premises. Have rents decreased in your area? Would your landlord like the hassle of having an empty property during a recession? If not, it could be a good time to review your rent when the contract expires.

Part 3: How to market your business

One of the things I've learned while running my own businesses is the importance of good marketing. Marketing simply means promoting and selling products or services, so the good news is that if you run your own business then by definition you must be involved in marketing – at least to some degree.

A business's first steps in marketing are often as simple as telling your friends and relatives that you're up and running and they can now buy whatever you have to offer. It might mean knocking on a few doors, or opening up your shop for the first time. Perhaps getting some signage or advertising your business telephone number. These are all solid foundations towards promoting what you do and therefore increasing the number of people that interact with you and the amount of money you make.

Once you realise you're doing marketing anyway, there are three secrets to taking your business marketing to a new level:

1. Understand how you're already marketing

What is it that you do that brings customers through your door week after week? Even if you're finding it tough to get customers right now, you had some in the past – so what brought them in? Is it your presence on a busy street, your shop signage or word of mouth that are bringing new customers in? Understanding where your customers are coming from can be as cheap and easy as asking them the simple question: "Where did you hear about my business?"

2. Find new and improved ways to market

You now understand what brings people in already, but are there other ways you could attract customers that wouldn't cost too much?

One reason that being able to identify new marketing opportunities is important is that you cannot assume a form of marketing that worked for you once will always continue to work in the future. For example, if you open a new shop you might expect to get some new customers as people become curious about what you do. But as time goes on, people's curiosity soon wanes and the amount of customers you get drops. Your existing marketing channel (having a shop premises on a busy street) is no longer effective.

But what else can you do to get more customers? How about an ad in the Yellow Pages, or perhaps distributing a leaflet with a map of how people can find your shop? How about something imaginative like giving out balloons or offering free product samples? Depending on your product or service, you might find internet marketing channels effective – for example, setting up a website or asking your friends to recommend you to others via Facebook or Twitter. You don't need to be an expert to begin using any of these forms of advertising as the costs can be very low indeed. So why not ask a business owner you know if they have tried any of these forms of marketing – and then give them a go for yourself!

3. Eliminate any ineffective ways of marketing that you pay for

One simple way to see if a form of marketing is effective is simply to keep a record of the dates when you distributed the leaflet or advertised in the Yellow Pages. Then compare your takings with the amount of money you made before you began using that form of marketing. If there is an increase, then maybe you've found a new way to market your business! The key, however, is to not spend any money on marketing activities that aren't increasing the amount of money you make in return.

So, in summary, if you want to increase the amount of customers you get, start by taking a hard look at what you do, spend a little money to see if you can find new ways of marketing and then cut back if they don't work.

Part 4: How to hire the right employee

Being your own boss definitely has its perks, especially when you're starting up a business. When I started out, I was driven by the freedom as well as the responsibility of working alone. But when my business began to grow, I realised how quickly there was profit to be made; the time came to employ the right people to help me on my journey to success.

It can be an expensive commitment to start paying another salary. So approach this carefully and with a lot of thought. Many of the first questions business owners will struggle with are simply who to hire, and when and where to find good, reliable candidates. Here is a rundown of some basic tips I found useful when I started hiring:

1. Where to start?

First you should assess: Do I really need to hire someone? You'll have to think about what jobs you can get done yourself and what you can get done by freelancers. Accounting, manufacturing, website design, marketing and public relations can all be completed by freelancers nowadays for a one-off payment. Deciding what to outsource and when to hire an employee will come down to whether you need continuous work on these areas or not.

2. Flexibility

Often, flexible candidates who are used to smaller environments are suited to smaller companies. Business owners want employees who can deal with multiple job roles without having their hand held. With your first hire, it will be tempting to pick a candidate with big-business credentials and experience on their CV. But think: Is this candidate a good fit for a small business?

Things like high salary expectations and benefits may be expected – something that many business owners can't commit to. I certainly couldn't when I began to hire. As a first hire in a growing business, employees may also not get a solid job title or role and may need to do a bit of everything.

Smaller businesses do have their perks, though! They are less bureaucratic and employees will find they have more breadth in their jobs than they usually do in big companies. Managers tend to have closer relationships with their employees and with this there is the potential for high growth within the business.

3. Networking

A great way to meet potential new employees is through networking. Ask your friends, family and industry colleagues for referrals or introductions. If they recommend somebody, they've helped you with some of the leg work by screening them. In my experience, if an employee recommends someone, there's a much higher likelihood that person will be successful in the job.

Why?

They get a more honest perspective of the company from the current employee, and in most cases an employee is only going to recommend someone they think will be successful, to avoid tarnishing their own reputation. At XLN we give our staff a bonus if they refer a friend who gets the job and completes their probation period. It's an easy and inexpensive way of recruiting the best people. But no matter how well-connected your employees are, eventually the internal network becomes exhausted.

4. Agencies

When the network runs dry, consider online job boards specific to the industry or job you are hiring for. Larger job boards like **Monster.com**, while having advantages, can bring down an avalanche of CVs on your head. And a smaller business will likely not have the time to sort through all of these.

Smaller sites can narrow your interested applicants to those in your industry or area. Also, keep an eye on blogs and websites in your industry. Some offer a place for help-wanted postings. Local newspapers and trade publications may also be useful sources, depending on your needs. Or if you're very pushed for time, recruiters can do all the legwork for you (for a fee).

*Christian Nellemann is CEO and founder of XLN
and a serial entrepreneur.*

WWW.XLN.CO.UK

Your Business in the Early Days – the Legals

by Susan Perry

1. Starting out

WHEN YOU'RE STARTING out you need good people around you. It doesn't have to be a full team of professional advisors, but you probably have people you know and trust with expertise and experience who can help you.

Whatever business structure you decide upon you will need to have a firm grip on the finances of your business, and trusted contacts to work with you on the accounting and tax issues you will face.

2. Getting other people involved – external investment / borrowing

To get your business going you are going to need money. You may have capital for starting out, but at some stage you are likely to need to build a relationship with your bankers.

If the terms are right, then an external investor could help drive your business forwards. This may be a simple cash injection, either by loan or for shares, though it could be more useful for the development of the company if the investor joins the board of directors and brings either skills in areas you don't already have covered or access to contacts who would otherwise be out of reach.

If you've ever watched the TV show *Dragons' Den* you will know that there is a balance to be struck between what the investor wants in return for their cash and what the founder of the business is prepared to give. It may be wonderful to get £100,000 and an expert on the board, but you may not want to give away 76% of your company in order to get it.

You should also watch out for people who want to take your equity and give you only their services in return. I have had lots of early-stage business people come to me who have been offered deals like this and they often aren't that attractive for the business in question.

After all, what is the point of bringing marketing and PR services into your business if you haven't got the cash flow to service the clients or fulfil the orders it will bring in?

3. Shareholders' agreements

If your company is owned by anyone other than just you, then I would urge you to consider a shareholders' agreement. There can be a lot going on in the early days and it is easy for a shareholders' agreement to get pushed down the list of priorities as something that is too time-consuming or expensive to deal with. But as the business develops and grows people can start to want different things, and that's when the trouble starts.

If you don't have a shareholders' agreement then you have to look to the Companies Act 2006 and the articles of association to govern the relationship between the shareholders. You could find out the hard way that something as basic as getting first refusal on the issue of new shares, or having the right to appoint a director, isn't covered.

Or, you might find that the provisions on share transfer in the articles of association make it impossible for you to sell your shares, even if you could find someone who wanted to buy a shareholding in a 50/50 deadlocked private company.

It is fairly standard for a shareholders' agreement to give the directors of a company in question day-to-day management of the business of the company, subject to a schedule of matters which are reserved to the shareholders.

Some matters, such as the issue of new shares or loan capital, may require the consent of all, or a high percentage, of shareholders. The reserved matters are key to the protection of the rights of each shareholder.

Others which are more closely linked to the running of the business could have approval set at a lower level; for example, making minor changes to a bank mandate, or altering the terms and conditions the business has with its customers.

Where shareholders are actively involved in the business as executive officers of the board there may be less concern, but where investors are bringing capital rather than management expertise the reserved matters are even more important for the protection of their investment.

4. Case study

Let's take a look now at a case study, based upon recent instructions in which I have been involved, where the client did not have a shareholders' agreement in place.

The company in question is involved in online retail, selling designer garden accessories. At the point I was instructed, the business had been trading for around three years.

There were two shareholders, each with 50% of the issued share capital of the company. The two shareholders were also the only two directors, though there was a company secretary as well, namely the father of one of the shareholders.

In the early days the directors were both actively involved in the running of the business, though each of them had day jobs while the venture was getting off the ground, which meant the time they could each devote to the company varied according to their other commitments.

Instead of buying a shelf company or incorporating a new one they used a company which the company secretary had previously been involved with and that had been dormant for a number of years.

The company had been incorporated prior to the Companies Act 1985 and the articles had never been changed.

As each of the shareholders got caught up in their other work commitments they communicated less and less about the business itself. Board meetings became less regular and one shareholder started to consult with the company secretary, his father, on matters concerning the business, rather than communicating with the other director.

The active director arranged for his amateur rugby team to be sponsored by the company, without consulting the other director or considering the impact on the brand.

It later transpired that financial records had not been properly kept, that expenses had been inflated and that stock had been stored in conditions which led to its deterioration and unsaleability.

Things came to a head when the active director approved final accounts at an inquorate board meeting, filed them at Companies House and refused to respond to the other director's requests for information and input.

The other director was also ejected from the company's premises when collecting stock to fulfil an order.

The excluded shareholder sought to involve a mutual friend in the role of arbitrator, but despite initial encouraging noises the uncooperative shareholder would not engage in the process.

With no shareholders' agreement and articles which were inadequate – and had been breached by the other director in any event – the long and painful way out of the situation was a negotiated solution where my client eventually bought out the other shareholder-director, but not without paying the price of a delay to the operation and growth of the business and not insignificant legal fees.

Of course not everyone is going to want to spend big on day one having bespoke articles and a full shareholders' agreement, but taking on a company which had previously traded with a long history largely unknown to the shareholders is likely to give hostage to fortune. Not least since on exit a purchaser would look to be indemnified for the prior period.

How could a shareholders' agreement have helped in this situation?

First, during the time that the shareholder-directors had commitments other than the company, it could have spelled out how much time each should be devoting each month to the business, as well as their roles within the business.

A shareholders' agreement could also have set out regular times and locations for board meetings and both that agreement and the articles could have permitted remote meetings by telephone or Skype.

A shareholders' agreement could also have provided for the form of financial information and the regularity with which it would be provided to shareholders, as well as setting out procedures for matters such as the process of claiming directors' expenses.

Matters relevant to branding could also be protected by a shareholders' agreement, so that sponsorship opportunities would be subject to shareholder approval and not left to the whim of one party.

When the dispute arose there was nothing but the articles to say what might happen next and going to the courts was something the client had neither the appetite nor the funds to contemplate.

A dispute or deadlock provision could have provided for independent arbitration that would have been binding on the parties.

The shareholders' agreement could have included provisions for the compulsory transfer of shares if a shareholder was in material and persistent breach and a procedure could have been put in place to give the shareholders a way to buy each other out.

5. Business basics – terms and conditions and making sure you get paid

As well as getting your internal relationships on to a firm footing, it's a good idea to think about how your business deals with the outside world.

Your terms of business should protect you, limit your liabilities and provide for payment. Your terms will depend on the nature of the business you are running and who your customers are. If you are dealing with consumers then there will be additional considerations and the terms will be slightly different if you are selling goods rather than services.

To consider all the possible terms for the different supplies would require a whole book, but I would like to flag a couple of issues about bringing standard terms into a contract with a customer and to give you some practical suggestions for making sure you get paid.

The first stage of forming a contract is the offer and acceptance. It is important that you bring your terms of business to the attention of your customer before the contract is formed. One way of doing this is to make sure that all pre-contract correspondence and documents are stated not to constitute offers – otherwise the contract may come into existence before you have put forward your standard terms.

So, make sure all brochures, emails and letters about possible orders or contracts state that they do not constitute an offer. You can also put a statement in your standard terms of business stating that any purchase order you receive from a customer will be an offer and that no contract will come into place until you have issued an acknowledgement of the order. If you have a standard order form make sure this refers to your terms of business and print them on the back.

On a practical level, some of the most important terms will be those relating to payment. Cash management and avoiding bad debtors is particularly important when a business is just starting, or when it is going through a period of rapid growth.

Your terms of business should include information on costs, delivery and your right to charge interest on late payments. If you are offering different payment options then these should also be set out here – for example, if you require a deposit before goods or services are provided, if you require payment in full in advance or if you are prepared to offer a discount for payment before the due date to encourage early payment and improve cash flow. If your standard terms are payment within 14 days of the date of the invoice then this should be stated – in your terms of business and on your invoices. Though bear in mind that larger customers may seek to impose their own payment terms on you with a longer period.

You may wish to consider sending invoices electronically and to accept payment by BACS or CHAPS bank transfer in order to speed up the process. Performing credit checks before entering into a larger contract can help reduce the credit risk you are exposed to and there are credit-monitoring services you can sign up to which can alert you when a customer may be becoming a greater credit risk.

Susan Perry is a Senior Associate solicitor at Kerman & Co LLP Solicitors.

WWW.KERMANCO.COM

Small Business and 'Bring Your Own Device': Bring it On

by Sarah Shields

E ACH YEAR, SMALL business owners are bombarded with a barrage of new acronyms and 'hot' tech trends to watch – some of which are more applicable to a small- and growing-business audience than others.

But 'Bring Your Own Device' – or BYOD – is not something they can dismiss as a buzzword irrelevant to their own organisations. In fact, with a massive 40% of British small business workers being able to choose the device they work on, compared with just 20% of large enterprise workers,[1] BYOD is perhaps even more of a reality for small businesses today than their larger counterparts.

The reality is that BYOD is pervasive, whether businesses like it or not, or have a BYOD policy in place. Employees are truly driving the change, with 37%[2] bringing non-compliant devices into their business networks before any formal policies are established. What's more, consumer appetite for such devices shows no signs of cooling; according to research from comScore,[3] more than six million people in the UK had a smartphone as well as a tablet in December 2012, and almost a third of all page views in the UK come from mobiles and tablets.

So what benefits could BYOD offer business? For smaller businesses, there is the clear IT infrastructure and cost rationalisation of allowing employees to use their own devices for business, but perhaps more significant is what BYOD promises in terms of productivity. A Dell Quest study into Global BYOD trends,[4] for example, found that 70% of companies believe BYOD improves employee productivity and customer response times. With the flexibility to use devices that best suit their preferred modes of working, employees have an opportunity to work more efficiently and creatively.

What's more, as the blurring of the private and business worlds continues, employees are going to demand more from IT, so there will be an increasing need for businesses to offer a culture of enablement, rather than one characterised by limitations. This may explain why 71% of organisations believe that implementing a BYOD policy improves workforce morale, while 65% recognise that it can be a valuable tool for attracting and retaining talent. These advantages can help a business to maintain its competitive advantage and avoid getting left behind – something which 59% of organisations feel could happen in the absence of a formal BYOD policy.

But the onslaught of multiple devices and operating systems means that businesses are grappling with the task of safely and securely enabling staff to create a personalised workspace that enhances the user experience and promotes productivity. There's no one-size-fits-all approach when it comes to BYOD policy, and virtually all policies are still maturing, but there are some key considerations:

- **Access rights and data security.** Data protection is the largest pain point for businesses grappling with BYOD. As privately owned tablets log on to corporate networks and exchange company files, it becomes harder for businesses to guarantee the accessibility, availability and protection of data stored beyond the confines of their infrastructures. IT must become an enabler, ensuring data is available, regardless of where and how it is stored and accessed. Business owners must account for company data that's out and about with an employee, ensuring its security when moving between secure corporate servers and unregistered personal devices.

- **Financial and management considerations.** The more devices accessing the likes of email and remote desktop, the more support issues come up and IT resources are stretched. A strict policy must be enforced to minimise these costs.

- **Accounting for the user.** It's a well-known fact that users themselves are the principal security risk within an organisation. Companies not only have to deal with people bringing in devices, but also other home-owned and managed applications and services as users demand a specific experience in their work environment. As time goes on, more devices, operating systems, services and apps will provide a growing number of interfaces with corporate data. A company must consider how it can implement policy-based user and content management to mitigate the risks.

So how can small businesses go about creating a BYOD policy that addresses these key considerations? Crucial to any successful policy is ensuring that an employee-centric approach is taken. Companies mustn't only consider productivity and cost-savings, but must ensure that users are comfortable in committing to a BYOD programme:

- **Make workflows simpler for employees**. Find and implement data solutions that help integrate personal device use and traditional IT without complicating workflows for employees. Use desktop virtualisation to enable users to access corporate content, personal content and external material in the same interface without jeopardising the integrity of corporate data from any location. Mobile device management systems (MDM) help a business to monitor when staff send/receive email, and access corporate data and external sites, dependent on how an employer configures their system. Staff must be comfortable with the way in which their personal devices are monitored for security; a balance between personal device and employer's rules must be struck.

- **Outline how devices may and may not be used** when connecting with company resources. Outline which operating systems, apps and sites will work, and those which may have limitations. Provide alternatives, not obstacles; prevent employees from using third-party business services such as Dropbox by providing employees with access to enterprise-friendly file-sharing tools.

- **Clearly detail the security requirements** for password protection, the rights of the company to lock or locate a lost device, and the level of reimbursement staff can expect for hardware costs and data usage. Penalties for failing to comply with security measures should be detailed.

- **Take a multi-layered approach to technology.** Combine numerous security technologies into a layered approach with proactive and reactive data protection. Include regular security audits to ensure mobile-related vulnerabilities are addressed and up-to-date.

- **Future-proof your business.** Update your business continuity plans to reflect BYOD realities; for example, detail ways to report lost devices so the company can cut access to company networks on a device.

Far from being a 'hot' business trend, BYOD is already happening in business, and those businesses that are able to approach it with preparation, the right technology and an open mind will be primed for success. Employee-driven change in the workforce is something that business owners ignore at their peril; correctly harnessed, it can be the lifeblood of thriving and competitive businesses.

Sarah Shields is General Manager and Executive Director of Consumer, Small and Medium Enterprises, Dell UK.

WWW.DELL.CO.UK

Notes

1. Dell and Intel Evolving workforce research: **www.dell.com/learn/us/en/ uscorp1/corp-comm/the-evolving-workforce?c=us&l=en&s=corp**

2. Forrester Fifteen Mobile Policy Best Practices: **www.scribd.com/doc/87883509/ Forrester-15-Mobile-Policy-Best-Practices**

3. Comscore 2013 Digital Future in Focus Series: **www.comscore.com/Insights/ Blog/2013_Digital_Future_in_Focus_Series**

4. Dell Quest survey of IT executives to gauge the level of organisational maturity with existing BYOD strategies: **www.quest.com/news-release/dell-unveils- global-byod-survey-results-embrace-byod-or-be-left-012013-819148.aspx**

Traits of Successful Entrepreneurs

by Peter Turner

IT IS IMPORTANT to map what a successful entrepreneur looks like to where they are in their business lifecycle. An entrepreneur in their first start-up has completely different characteristics to an entrepreneur who has been trading for 3–4 years or more, or a serial entrepreneur, especially if they are well-funded.

The main characteristic of great entrepreneurs is that they adapt, change and become great leaders as their businesses grow. They have a great vision, they can inspire people, are very focused on having a well-run business and they understand their business and their markets. They are often driven and focused.

I was recently told that statistics show that only 5% of all British starts-ups grow beyond £5m turnover, and of those only 10% grow beyond £10m turnover. I meet over 200 businesses a year, of which 2–3 are or will grow beyond £10m turnover. I see numerous businesses that are between £4m and £8m turnover, whose revenues have stalled and profits have declined, and I see numerous businesses whose turnover is between £2m and £4m who are heading straight towards the same position as those above.

Great entrepreneurs will grow revenue into the tens of millions. So what differentiates them from the rest and how can you adopt such principles into your business?

At every stage of a business lifecycle, the best entrepreneurs are focused on four key areas ...

1. Vision

A vision is important because it describes what you are going to do and sets the framework for how you employ, focus, motivate and measure people as your business grows. If you already employ people, a clear vision focuses their minds and enables your staff to contribute more.

Don't get too caught up in creating the best vision possible. What you need is a *working* vision for where you are in your business cycle; this can change over the years.

As a start-up, the vision could be quite specific: 'We are going to sell our product direct to consumers between 30 and 50 years of age'. As your business grows this could become more general, describing your long-term vision. At a business I managed (£6m turnover) we decided our vision was to sell to just 50 clients. Today, that business has a turnover in excess of £80m, with considerable profits. But that narrow, concrete vision gave us a very clear direction when we needed it and made decisions easier.

While working on your vision, take time to understand your customer base (be quite specific here; you can often double turnover inside a business by reducing the width of your current clients) and your routes to market. The great entrepreneurs always look for ways that will enable their business to scale. This will mostly be how marketing works, aligned with the sales team.

2. People

People are the most important part of your business. They are the key to success and fortune, to failure and grief. The workforce today is so different to ten years ago; technology, mobility and a wealth of expertise available on a part-time basis means entrepreneurs can up-skill their business considerably quicker and cheaper than previously.

However, unless your staff are mapped to your vision and there is a clear brief and expectation of what you want them to achieve and how you want them to perform, great performance is unlikely.

Effective employment starts with understanding your vision and thinking long term. Make use of an HR consultant who can think strategically and can help you build a scalable organisational structure.

Once you know your organisational structure, build a profile analysis of the people you want in each role. You may have them already, but this exercise is really important if you want to grow – it may highlight areas of training for your existing staff.

Seek to build a great team of individuals. Again, this starts with having a vision and people knowing where they fit within that. You need to build a culture of trust and openness. Develop other leaders in your business at all levels.

Invest in yourself to become a great leader – nothing will motivate and drive performance more than you becoming a great leader. Five per cent of entrepreneurs don't need training in this, 95% do! Do not be afraid to build a support team for you; the best entrepreneurs do. Remember that nothing will motivate the business more than you being a great leader.

3. Processes

Great entrepreneurs are process-driven. All you need to do is look at how they manage their time to realise that without structure, process and clarity they could not achieve what they achieve. It may sound like losing entrepreneurship, or the ability to be flexible and take advantage of opportunities or change as required, but strong processes actually strengthen the business, make decision-making easier and empower everyone in the business at all levels. Excellent processes also make it a more pleasurable experience for your customers, your staff and other external parties you deal with.

Processes should cover all areas of your business. You should have a process for what happens when you make a sale, a customer returns a product, staff reviews, what reporting you want inside the business, how to manage salespeople, how to run a board meeting, etc.

The more you put processes into your business, the easier decision-making will be and the faster your business will grow.

4. Management

Management must be consistent and fair. You can have a hard management style but it must always be fair. You may have an amazing motivational environment, but you must have rules and there must be protocols for when those rules are not adhered to.

Steve Kelly, a very successful businessman, would hold a monthly meeting with his direct reports – he was very clear on appraisal or reprimand. However, if during the month someone breached the rules or he had something on his mind, he would immediately talk to his staff about the issue. He never wanted his staff to think something he wasn't thinking, or for them to accept poor performance or to step out of line.

For management to be effective you need to ensure people know what is expected of them; clarity is so important. That is not to say that you want people to become robots or unthinking. The total opposite is true: people can add more value because they are *focused*.

Management is about expectations – and great leaders set some for themselves too. Top business leaders are constantly looking at how to improve their performance. This cannot be done unless you have a benchmark.

Business lifecycle

The key to success is how you react to changes in your business lifecycle. There are three stages:

1. zero to £3m turnover

2. £4m to £10m turnover

3. £10m+.

In this article I am only going to talk about businesses in the £4m-to-£10m turnover stage. Businesses below this threshold should be able foresee the issues they will face as they become a larger business.

The £4m-to-£10m turnover stage is where the good entrepreneurs become leaders. In other words:

- They understand their vision, employ the right people and empower and motivate them. They are focused on building up teams of individuals rather than just individuals.

- They know what organisational structure they need.

- They seek to build a high-performance team and are not afraid to employ great people.

- They build strong processes into their businesses.

- The entrepreneur develops excellent communication skills, spends a lot of time with the people inside the business and becomes knowledgeable about their staff, how to communicate with them and how they like to be communicated to.

- The entrepreneur is the leader, at the forefront of the tough decisions and making the strategic choices; they are thinking long term, while monitoring the short term. They are clear about their work and the business because both are mapped to a precise vision.

- Their expectations on deliverables increases and they set clear roadmaps on performance expectations. Additionally they do not shy away from managing people who are underperforming.

Successful entrepreneurs make decisions. They have a support team around them; they listen, they want to be better. They remove themselves from the day-to-day work but are still involved – the difference being that they get things done through people rather than doing it themselves. They sell their thoughts rather than yell at people.

Average performing businesses in this business lifecycle stage all too often lack the competency to understand where their business is, where it should go and how to get it there. They lack management skills and often accept average performance.

It is often hard work for entrepreneurs to get to this stage in the first place. And when they first enter it they are making good profits. Some therefore start increasing the cost-base of the business and begin taking large dividends. Then after 2–4 years, revenues slow. The skill-sets required to manage a larger business don't exist, haven't been acquired or invested in through training, and everything has drifted. It's a larger business being run like a small one.

The key for success in this business lifecycle stage is to ensure you, the entrepreneur, as the leader of the business develop your leadership skills and build a strong executive team around you.

I would start with a strong finance director, these can be part-time. Then I would seek to employ a strong sales director, followed by someone with strategic HR skills (part-time), before building out marketing and operations. This may change slightly depending on the industry.

The people you bring on board should be able to help you develop your leadership skills.

*Peter Turner is a Regional Director at the FD Centre
and founder of the Entrepreneurs' Club, London.*

WWW.THEFDCENTRE.CO.UK

WWW.ENTREPRENEURSCLUBLONDON.COM

A Trusted Business Advisor Entrepreneurs Can Count On

by Hartmut Wagner

S MALL AND MEDIUM-sized businesses dominate the British business landscape. At the last count, there were 4.8 million small firms registered in the UK, representing 99.9% of all businesses in the country and employing around 24 million people. That figure looks set to keep growing.

While the public sector has shed thousands of jobs, the private sector – dominated by these huge numbers of SMEs – continues to shrug off some of the challenges thrown up by the tough economic environment, and continues to create employment and training opportunities. Perhaps unsurprisingly optimism is running high, particularly among entrepreneurs.

According to the latest business growth survey by Santander, SMEs are predicting their highest growth in the last three years. They are expecting to grow an average 134% over the next five years – up from 88% in 2012 and 104% in 2011. Wales and the South West are expected to see a particularly rosy future, with growth figures of 300% forecast over that period.

One of the biggest legacies these new-breed of SMEs and entrepreneurs have introduced into this new-look economy is a 'can-do' attitude, where people young and old aren't afraid of asking themselves how they can turn their passions and skills into business ideas. On the back of that entrepreneurial spirit, there are now on average more than 2,500 businesses start-ups springing into life each and every day in the UK.

There are many theories in the media as to why more people than ever are 'giving it a go', including the poor state of the economy and lack of jobs; the fact that millennials are turning away from traditional organisations and career paths; the growth in government support for small businesses; and the rise of high-profile entrepreneurs. But whatever the reason behind this trend, it has brought about a new way of working that presents exciting opportunities for those involved – along with some interesting challenges.

SMEs hampered by poor internal processes

While this newfound enthusiasm for business and entrepreneurialism is admirable and, indeed, crucial to the economic recovery, we have found that many SMEs are hampering their own progress by using poor internal systems. These systems are not fully supporting their particular needs and are causing unnecessary wastage. Independent research, commissioned by Exact, shows that collectively the UK's SMEs could be losing out to the tune of £3.7 billion or more as a result of inefficient processes.

Among the most startling findings was that 20% of SMEs admit to having forgotten to invoice for goods or services at least once. Among these, around 12% confess to not invoicing for a job worth between £5,000 and £10,000, while 6% admit to having forgotten to invoice for a job worth more than £10,000.

These findings are particularly concerning when you consider that growth appears to be the primary focus point for many entrepreneurs, and keeping on top of cash flow is a central part of achieving such growth. The survey, by way of confirmation, showed the biggest cause of stress among SMEs is fighting for new business (31%), closely followed by worries over finances (23%), such as cash flow issues, debtors and business planning.

Widespread concern over cash flow

But why should cash flow be such an issue for SMEs? By the very nature of their size, SMEs have the means to be more nimble than their larger counterparts, often giving them a vital competitive edge to seize on opportunities as and when they manifest themselves.

Take a small retailer, for example. A shop owner may choose to differentiate themselves on price and will undoubtedly as a result be constantly on the lookout for competitively priced stock options. So if a large amount of cheap stock is unexpectedly being offloaded, the retailer needs to be able to react quickly and grab that chance when it arises. Knowing what their cash flow situation is, and whether they can afford to commit to that opportunity at any given time, is a vital part of an SME's business success.

Entrepreneurs need to be in control of their business and finances at all times in order to fulfil their firms' growth potential. Unfortunately a great many fall short. The Exact research, which was commissioned to get a better understanding of the working relationships and processes in place between SMEs and their accountants, shows that 25% of business owners and leaders admit that they don't feel fully in control of their accounts and business finances. These shortcomings also appear to have a wider impact on their businesses; nearly half (45%) of SMEs say they have had to defer payments of one kind or another due to cash flow problems, including failing to pay staff wages on time. Of these, 27% failed to pay suppliers on time at some point; 14% failed to pay fixed bills (such as utilities, phone and rent), and 12% have failed to pay staff wages on time.

Getting into the mindset of entrepreneurs

Having total control over your business and finances is essential. However, our research again suggests that working practices and the processes used by many SMEs at present don't always support that necessity. Part of this has to boil down to the fact that some of these systems don't take into account the mindset and behaviour of this particular breed of business leader. Entrepreneurs tend to be confident, fast-paced, enthusiastic individuals with tunnel-like vision in their pursuit of their goals. They live life in the here-and-now, but with their eyes very much fixed on the future, looking for opportunities and ready to jump on those opportunities as they fly in. Having real-time access and up-to-date information about their business and finances is therefore key to supporting their forward-looking needs and expectations.

Our research shows one-third (33%) of SMEs use Excel spreadsheets or paper records as part of their accounting processes, and only 14% are using cloud-based accounting systems – something that accountants (86%) believe can carry a huge number of benefits for SMEs, and for a number of different reasons. Entrepreneurs, with their go-get-'em approach, are notoriously time poor, and often work on the go, working remotely to ensure the maximum use of their time. Not surprisingly, traditional business and finance management solutions that don't involve the cloud can struggle to cope with this dynamic business model. Entrepreneurs cannot wait, for example, for their accountant to get into the office and process information that may be weeks old, before feeding information back to them which is too late to act on. Using a cloud-based solution means they have sight of their finances at anytime, anywhere, and can base business decisions on accurate, up-to-date information, rather than on assumptions or data that is yet to be properly processed.

Business leaders demanding big picture insights

At the same time as wanting access to information 'right now', SMEs also want access to more of it. Market research gathered from a number of our own focus groups shows SMEs are increasingly demanding richer information that provides visibility of their entire business, not just their accounts. They want to feel more in control over all their business functions with a bigger picture view of their KPIs, such as costs, debtors and profits. And not just that – they want more from the people traditionally seen as the gate-keepers of that information; their accountants. Entrepreneurs are no longer looking for accountants to just sort out the books – they are looking for a trusted advisor, who can provide holistic financial and strategic support, based around their vision for growth.

This change in relationship, with accountants no longer being seen as just bean counters, appears to be on a good footing. According to the Exact research, more than half of SME leaders trust their accountant more than anyone else when it comes to broader business issues, including their own business partners (38%) or friends in similar businesses (35%). Interestingly, they trust their spouses or partner more to offer them business advice (29%) than their bank manager (18%).

Accountants regarded as SMEs' most trusted advisors

This level of trust appears to be reciprocated by accountants, with over half of those polled in the survey saying they feel they hold some sway and influence over their SME clients' broader business decision-making. But while levels of trust between the two parties seem to be high, the lines of communication don't always appear to be good enough to support that relationship, particularly given the fast pace of business today.

The vast majority of accountants (61%) communicate with their SME clients no more than once a month. So while SMEs are placing more and more faith in their accountants to provide big picture business advice, in a large proportion of cases that appears to be fulfilled only on a limited basis.

To really utilise the skills and value-added services that an accountant can bring to SMEs to the full – and really utilise them as trusted business advisors – entrepreneurs need to ensure the correct processes and systems are being used, which enable accountants to access their business and financial information more easily and more frequently. This is something only a cloud-based software solution can provide.

Cloud holds answer to greater collaboration

Among the main benefits cited by accountants for using cloud-based business and finance software is being able to have greater visibility of clients' financial information, followed closely by the opportunity to spot issues while they can still be resolved.

This ability to identify any potential issues, which a good software solution can flag automatically, means damaging issues can be avoided before they arise, including things like invoices slipping unnecessarily through the system.

But the benefits of an online business and finance software solution to SMEs don't just stop there. Accountants polled in the Exact research study also highlighted that there is less opportunity for human error, meaning data is more accurate, along with the means to be able to collaborate with clients on the same set of data. For accountants that means having a multi-layered view of their clients' business and financial records and activities in real-time, with the right kind of software, like Exact Online (**www.exactonline.co.uk**), allowing them to analyse any underperforming areas of their business by sector or region, so that they can truly provide up-to-date holistic business and financial advice as expected by their SME clients.

A recent report by the Federation of Small Businesses presents a powerful case for the cloud and the benefits it can bring SMEs. It reads:

> "In tough economic times small businesses in the UK need to be innovative and efficient to survive and grow. To do this, small businesses need to make the best possible use of the technology available to them. The good news is there are lots of opportunities. Whether through enabling e-commerce, new ways of marketing or improving the efficiency of internal processes – technology offers small businesses many ways to boost their performance."

It warns, however, that this message is failing to filter through to the vast majority of entrepreneurs, finding that only one-quarter of small firms are actually investing in technology such as cloud computing in general, meaning many of them are missing out on powerful ways to access a global customer base as well as dramatically improve efficiency and customer service.

We live in an entrepreneurial age, and the UK is very much at the forefront of that trend. With it comes a view of a new way of doing business. SMEs operate in an often fiercely competitive and rapidly changing marketplace and the need to stay one step ahead of the curve requires a different approach to business and finance planning. It requires having access to a deeper, more holistic view of their business, with better channels of communication in place between them and their most trusted advisor, their accountant. This is a particularly exciting time to be bringing our cloud portfolio to the UK. Never has there been a greater need for the two sides to collaborate more effectively and we at Exact are going to be doing our part to support this evolution.

Hartmut Wagner is Managing Director of
Cloud Solutions at Exact.

WWW.EXACT.COM

The Importance of Enterprise Education

by Alice Barnard

WHAT DO YOU get when you combine the potential of enterprise with the power of education? The answer is a potentially life-changing combination that might just have the ability to achieve something amazing.

Right now there are nearly a million young people out of work, and yet businesses of all sizes report huge difficulties in recruiting young people with the skills they need to help them grow. The fact is, there is an enormous gap between the kind of skills that young people can offer and the skills and abilities that employers need. Whether it's basic communication skills, sales experience, marketing expertise or sound financial understanding, it's obvious that thousands of young people lack the fundamental employability skills required by businesses today.

Clearly there is a problem. The old way of doing things is not working. We need to explore new ways of doing things, which is where enterprise education comes in. Enterprise education is essentially the art of equipping young people still at school or college with the business and entrepreneurial skills they need to be able to succeed in the real world of work. It is a crucial piece of the jigsaw that could go a long way to redress the current mismatch between young people's abilities and employers' needs.

Of course, none of us know what the job situation will look like in five years' time, let alone in ten or 20 years' time. Factors such as advances in technology, increasing population size and people working longer into retirement age mean that the nature of employment and the workplace, and with it the type of skills and abilities that will be required, are changing so fast that it would take a brave person to predict the future. But what we do know is that young people will need to be increasingly flexible and adaptable to be able to rise to meet the challenges of this changing workplace, whether that is working for someone else or creating their job by starting up their own business.

The concept of a job for life is long gone and even the idea of permanent full-time employment is changing. Instead young people are likely to find themselves pursuing multifaceted portfolio careers, which may encompass anything from undertaking a succession of short-term projects, to doing several jobs at once, to periods of working for other people interspersed with periods of working for themselves.

It is our belief at the Peter Jones Foundation that the best way forward is to equip young people with an entrepreneurial mindset so that they can apply the tools and insights of an entrepreneur to every aspect of their working lives, whether they end up working for themselves or for someone else. Thinking like an entrepreneur can give a young person not only the essential business tools they need to progress, but also the self-confidence and belief they will need to succeed in a competitive marketplace.

We are convinced that the best way of equipping young people with these essential skills is through the concept of 'learning by doing', so that real learning is done in real business situations and therefore becomes entirely intuitive.

The Peter Jones Foundation, which was set up by entrepreneur Peter Jones CBE in 2005, provides enterprise education in two different ways. The first is through our programme Tycoon in Schools, a three-month competition for 11–18 year olds which teaches enterprise skills in schools through learning by doing. This year more than 250 secondary schools nationwide have entered the competition, which gives young people the opportunity to have a go at starting a real business for themselves. Students work together in teams to come up with a winning business idea, which is pitched to a panel of judges. The best proposals receive a start-up loan from the Peter Jones Foundation – up to £1,000 per school – to launch their ventures, which the young people run as a real business for four weeks. During this time the business will be judged on innovation, performance and profits.

Last year young people taking part in the competition came up with an impressive range of innovative business ideas, from handcrafted clothing exchanges and community-written recipe books, to customised technology accessories. At the end of the competition students repay the loan and remaining profits can be reinvested into their business, given to their school or donated to local charitable causes.

It's a simple idea, but it is proving to be extremely effective on many levels. The Tycoon in Schools programme not only engages students who are keen to learn, but has been incredibly successful in engaging those students who, for whatever reason, struggle to stay focused at school. It was discovered last year, for example, that students who had been persistently truanting were turning up to school every day for the three months that Tycoon in Schools was running, so that they could get involved, such was their passion for the project.

The Peter Jones Foundation is also providing enterprise education to young people through the Peter Jones Enterprise Academy, a nationwide programme run within existing further education colleges. The academy was started in 2009 and offers five different courses in enterprise and entrepreneurship for students of 16 years old and above, including two which lead to BTEC qualifications and two apprenticeships which enable students to earn while they learn.

The central focus of every course is to equip future entrepreneurs with the entrepreneurial skills and mindset they need to either run their own businesses or to work for an established organisation, where they can add real value and offer new, innovative strategies. Our courses are focused on a 'learning by doing' approach. Our staff posses real business knowledge and combine innovative teaching methods with sessions from industry experts to provide the best possible experience for our young entrepreneurs. Firms such as Grant Thornton and the Chartered Institute of Purchase and Supply offer not only their time but also real-life business expertise, national business challenges and job opportunities to our network of students and graduates. The academy also works closely with many successful entrepreneurs from all areas of business, who come in to deliver masterclasses and entrepreneurial talks to the students.

The fact is that enterprise education at any level is an incredible enabler. It helps young people to think more freely, and it opens up their minds to all kinds of exciting opportunities and possibilities. It gives them self-confidence and self-awareness and enables them to develop key academic skills such as literacy and numeracy because they are using these skills intuitively in a 'learning by doing' environment. If young people taking part in the Tycoon in Schools programme have to create a marketing poster or sales literature to persuade customers to buy their products, for example, they will be using key English skills almost without noticing – and they will be trying their best because they own the business and it matters to them.

Enterprise education fulfils another vital function, by showing young people what options could be possible in their lives. Schools are no longer required to provide independent careers advice to help students make decisions about their next steps, whether that is to higher education, or a job, or another path. This means that young people can find it hard to find the information and role models they need to help them make the right decisions. Tycoon in Schools plays an important role in showing young people the range of employment options open to them, whether that be working for a large or small business or opting to start one of their own. For many young people simply realising that they could effectively create their own job by starting a business is an immensely exciting and empowering idea.

It is important to start this process at a young age. Research studies suggest that young people, particularly girls, make decisions about their future careers incredibly early, often as young as ten. That means that as they move up through school they are already starting to narrow their choices and their options, often without realising it.

Despite the obvious importance of enterprise education to young people, however, without initiatives such as Tycoon in School it can be hard for schools to know how to go about providing it. There is little or no government funding to schools for the provision of enterprise education and it has been sidelined in the national curriculum. It can be hard for schools, which intuitively recognise the importance of enterprise education, to overcome the twin obstacles of lack of funding and lack of priority in order to make enterprise education a reality. School heads have to be dynamic and forward-thinking to stand up and say they think enterprise education is important for their young learners and that it has broader benefits for their education and progression through life, and many do.

We recognise this, and so one of our tasks at the Peter Jones Foundation is to help make it easier for schools to incorporate enterprise education into what they offer by providing them with the tools, resources and support they need through Tycoon in Schools.

The fact is that enterprise education is important, not just for the individual students themselves, but for the wider economy as a whole. Equipping young people with entrepreneurial skills and an entrepreneurial mindset not only creates a future generation of entrepreneurs who will be able to set up their own businesses, which will in turn create employment opportunities for others and regenerate local communities; it also equips young people with the personal skills they need to be better and more effective employees. That is great news for any business owner, because building a base of brilliant employees who can bring ideas and inspiration is crucial for the growth of their enterprise. Without a solid group of skilled workers that can be relied upon to get the best results, and deliver them consistently, making a success of their company will prove difficult.

There is no getting away from the size of the problem. With nearly one million young people out of work in Britain, as a nation we are in danger of losing an entire generation of young people who will simply fall through the gaps of society unless something is done. It is this we are tackling here at the Peter Jones Enterprise Academy.

Young people are a fantastic business asset – they bring energy, passion and new approaches to challenges, as well as the ability to spot opportunities through fresh thinking. There are many young people across the UK who have the potential to achieve highly, in whatever field they go in to. We just need to ensure that they are provided with the necessary tools, support and encouragement to enable them to make the most of what they have to offer and achieve their goals.

The bottom line is that enterprise education has the ability to transform individual lives, to transform businesses, and ultimately to transform the fortunes of Britain.

Alice Barnard is Chief Executive of the Peter Jones Foundation.

WWW.PETERJONESFOUNDATION.ORG

An Introduction to Personal Brand Mapping

by Allan Biggar

YOUR BRAND IS the shorthand description of you and what you do. Your brand is what people say about you when you are not in the room. Everyone is a brand!

Over the 25 years I've advised business leaders, entrepreneurs and politicians, I've seen most situations. Brand Me© represents the lessons I've learned brought together in a tool created to help individuals in leadership positions understand, create and manage their personal brand. This chapter aims to guide you through the Brand Me© method process.

The process helps to:

- create a road map to success

- set your objectives

- define barriers and drivers which may help or impede you

- set communications objectives.

Your personal brand: why is it important?

Personal branding is how we market ourselves to others. The reasons why personal branding has always existed is that we always have to sell ourselves in various situations, from trying to impress our managers to meeting new friends. Also, we're always being judged based on first impressions. From the clothing you wear, to how you behave and interact with other people, everything is tied in to your overall brand.

Corporations act like individuals because consumers demand brand engagement and two-way conversations. That's why you see employees tweeting and updating their status messages under a corporate umbrella. The same strategies companies use to brand products can be leveraged to brand people, such as blogging, search engine optimisation, and press releases.

Your personal brand is everything. It's your reputation, the size and strength of your network, and what unique value you bring.

Your personal brand: what are the benefits from managing your brand?

Just like corporate brands, people can demand a premium price (a higher salary) based on their brand value. Coca-Cola is more expensive than a supermarket brand, yet it tastes similar. Consumers are willing to pay more for Coca-Cola because of the strength of its brand.

Another benefit is that you will become more visible to your peers, hiring managers, other successful business people and entrepreneurs. With visibility comes jobs, clients, celebrity-status and the opportunity to make a difference! People will want to work with you, or work for you!

The network that you develop because of your brand can also protect you from today's uncertain work environment and allow you to grow your business.

Why should entrepreneurs care about personal branding?

Venture capitalists, angel investors and partners want to work with strong personal brands that have successful track records.

Your personal brand is transferable, so if your business fails, you don't have to start from scratch again. People are searching for you, or people like you, online, and if you don't have a solid brand presence, you won't be taken seriously.

A lot of entrepreneurs, especially internet entrepreneurs, have to build large networks before they generate media and investor attention.

Getting started

Discover: In order to really understand who you are, investing in self-discovery is critical. In fact, if you don't spend time learning about yourself, your personal mission, and unique attributes you will be at a disadvantage when marketing your brand to others.

Start by asking yourself 'What do I want to be known for?' Create a personal mission statement; it might include the following …

I will:

- use my talents as a communicator to teach others

- use my social skills to bring people closer together

- be inspired by the smallest of challenges

- live in awe of my good fortune in life.

Create: Your personal branding toolkit may consist of a blog, website, business card, CV, video CV, reference document, cover letter, portfolio, social network profile or a combination of these. Your brand must be consistent and reinforce each part of your toolkit.

Communicate: There are five steps to branding everything you've created to let people know you exist. You can communicate your brand by attending professional networking events, writing articles for magazines and media sites, commenting on blogs, connecting with people on social networks and reaching out to the press.

Maintain: As you grow and accelerate in your career, everything you've created has to be updated and accurately represent the current 'brand you'. Also, you need to monitor your brand online to ensure all conversations about you are positive and factual. You can do this by using a combination of tools, including a Google Alert for your name.

The Brand Me© method

Your brand for the future: Brand takes reputation a step further. Branding means demonstrating and aggressively promoting what you're known for. Essentially, it takes your reputation to a higher level of awareness and publicity. The following steps will take you through the Brand Me© method to help create your brand.

Identify what you value: Your personal brand is ultimately a reflection of everything you value. For example, if you value honesty, then your brand will most likely reflect the way you're always honest with your clients and prospects. Or if you value knowledge, then your brand will most likely incorporate the way you acquire, use and communicate information.

So take time to really think about the things you value in your life. List them. Make sure the values you identify are truly your own because you must believe in and live by them every day. These values will become the foundation for your brand, as well as your personal mission statement. They will help you align yourself and everything you do with what you choose to stand for.

Identify what makes you unique: With your values as your foundation, the next step is to determine your specific uniqueness. Everyone is unique and special in some way. For example, maybe you are the only salesperson on your team with children. In this case, you can relate to other parents on a different level than anyone else in your company. Or maybe you are the only one with a background in technology, so you know exactly how to meet the needs of people in that industry.

How are you different as an individual? How are you unique? How are your products and services different? Incorporate this uniqueness into your brand.

Identify how you want to be perceived: Branding is about other people's perceptions of you. You have the power to control most of these perceptions with your actions and presentation. Obviously, some people simply won't like you and others will be jealous of you. But you can control most perceptions.

Consider how you want to be perceived in your clients' and prospects' minds. Whether you like it or not, you already have a reputation with the people you know. Maybe you're branded as the slob in the group, or the big mouth; whatever it is, you have a brand. Now you need to decide if you like that brand. Ask yourself, 'Is this the brand I want?' If not, are you willing to make the commitment to do something about it? You have to want the prize and be willing to do the work to attain it.

Identify your speciality: Next, consider what speciality you want to be known for and take action to achieve it. If you want to be branded as a great public speaker, then you have to pay your dues and join a relevant association, hire coaches, take constructive criticism, get up and talk, and work your way through that crowd. If you want to be branded as the best value-added salesperson, then you have to bring extra value to every client or prospect meeting. Your prospects might not always like the particular ideas you bring each time they meet with you, but they will take your calls and meet with you because they know they can expect new and valuable ideas from you. When you're consistent with your speciality, everyone will know you for it.

Identify your target market: The goal of branding is to build customer loyalty. As you're creating your brand, you need to determine your target market and speak directly to them. For example, if you sell mini-vans, then you might target mothers with three or more children in your brand. But if you sell pick-up trucks, then you will obviously need to speak to a completely different audience.

Also, you want your target audience to feel they really need your expertise.

In other words, you don't want them to say, "She's good". Instead you want them to say, "I've got to have *her* as an advisor!" You want people to think that your brand will make a difference in their lives, so it must be meaningful to the end user. And it must create a vivid picture in their mind of results and guaranteed satisfaction. Essentially your brand is a trust label, and loyalty comes from that trust.

Write your brand: Now that you know all the elements that form your brand, you have to actually write the brand's statement – a phrase that jumps out at you from the page and grabs your emotions. Start by incorporating at least one action verb. Then keep it short and simple. You want to make it unique, memorable and repeatable.

You also want it to ring an emotional bell that causes clients and prospects to focus on you, and you alone, when they need your type of service (i.e. *Action Jackson gets results*).

Visualise, walk and talk your brand: Finally, once you have created your brand, you must publicise it. Start acting out your brand immediately. Tell others about it and ask them to spread the word. Establish a group of advocates who understand you and can publicise your brand to all the people they know. This will create word-of-mouth buzz. You don't want to let these people go too long without hearing from you.

Also, circulate your brand by publishing articles, collecting testimonials from clients and creating a tagline that goes with what you are. You want to make yourself as visible as possible. So be able to describe your business succinctly, speak in front of people, have a presence, and most importantly, be consistent with your brand.

Now set your career and personal objectives

Having spent time developing your brand we now need to see how that applies to helping you meet your own personal, career, business, financial and any other objectives you may have.

To do this, set yourself 'SMART' goals. That is, goals which are:

• Specific, Measureable, Achievable, Realistic and Time-based.

Let's break this down word by word …

Be specific

To make a goal achievable, you need to clearly define your target or end result. *Specifics* are key! A vague goal is hard to achieve. It also needs to be a big enough goal to keep your motivation up throughout the process. Start out with a clear direction and focus for your objective. An easy way to define specifics is to think of the 5 Ws (and 1 H):

- **Who:** Who will be involved?

- **What:** What am I looking to accomplish?

- **Where:** Identify a location for your goal.

- **When:** What is the time frame for my goal?

- **Why:** What is the purpose of the goal? What are the benefits if I accomplish it?

- **How:** What are the means for accomplishing the goal?

Make it measurable

How will you determine if you've achieved your goal? Even if it's a tough thing to measure, you need to make your goal *measurable* in some way. For example, a goal of weight loss can be measured by pounds and inches lost from your body. However, other goals are less quantifiable. For goals that are tough to measure, develop a ranking system in order to keep track of progress. Make adjustments if you realise something is not working.

Focus on actions

To keep yourself on track, develop a plan of action for *achieving* your goal. At first, a general outline is adequate. As you start making changes to achieve your goal, make your plan very specific to continue pushing yourself toward the end result.

Be realistic

Your goal needs to be something that is possible to achieve. All too often people put unnecessary amounts of pressure on themselves to make drastic changes in the New Year. A goal can always evolve once you've achieved the initial result. It also needs to be something that's in your control!

Stick to a time-bound schedule

Deadlines are important – after all, how often would something be put off if it didn't have a deadline? Achieving a goal can become almost impossible if you do not put an end date on it. You'll find yourself putting it off or making excuses instead of pushing toward positive change.

SMART goals can help you on your path to success – and so can HARD goals. This tactic, coined by Mark Murphy in *Hard Goals: The Secrets to Getting from Where You Are to Where You Want to Be* (McGraw-Hill, 2010), taps into an individual's emotional, visual, survival, and learning systems – enabling them to visualise what they need to achieve.

HARD goals are:

- Heartfelt: Develop deep-seated and heartfelt attachments to your goals on levels that are intrinsic, personal and extrinsic. Use these connections to naturally increase the motivational power you put behind making your goals happen.

- Animated: Create goals that are vividly alive in your mind. Use visualisation and imagery to sear your goal firmly into your brain including perspective, size, colour, shape, distinct parts, setting, background, lighting, emotions and movement.

- **R**equired: Give procrastination the boot. Convince yourself and others of the absolute necessity of your goals and make the future payoffs of your goals appear far more satisfying than what you can get today. This will amp up your urgency to get going on them right now.

- **D**ifficult: Construct goals that are optimally challenging to tap into your own personal sweet spot of difficulty. Access past experiences to use them to position you for extraordinary performance. Identify your goal-setting comfort zone and push past it in order to attain the stellar results you want.

Putting it all together

- For each objective we need to create a plan.

- We need to map out the key events in those plans on an integrated map.

- We need to set milestones and key events.

- We need to think about resources needed to make each plan happen.

- We need to think about what might happen to speed things up, slow things down or change objectives all together.

- Now create a time line.

Your personal branding kit

Now that you know what you want to do and have claimed a niche, it's time to get it on paper and online. The sum of all the marketing material you should develop for your brand is called a **Personal Branding Kit**. This kit consists of the following elements that you can use to highlight your brand and allow people to easily view what you're about:

1. **Business card:** Everyone should have their own business card. The card should contain your picture, your personal brand statement (such as *"Lincolnshire financial expert"*), as well as your preferred contact information and corporate logo if necessary.

2. **CV/cover letter/references document:** These are typical documents that you need for applying for jobs and when you go on interviews (something over two million job seekers will be doing as we speak). Be sure to prioritise each document with information customised to the target position. Take your CV online and add social features to it to make the ultimate social media CV, promoting your personal brand to the world and making it shareable.

3. **Portfolio:** Whether you use a CD, web or print portfolio, it's a great way to showcase the work you've done in the past. A top portfolio can convince someone of your ability to accomplish the same results for the future. **Figdig.com** and **carbonmade. com** are social networks for people who want to show off their creative skills to the world.

4. **Blog/website:** Depending on who you are, you should either start a blog or stick with a static homepage. Those who blog will have a stronger asset than those who don't because blogs rank higher in search engines and help establish your expertise and interest areas over time. Also critical is interaction with other blogs. You may soon find yourself being quoted and perhaps asked to guest blog. If not, reach out and ask to guest blog; you'll be surprised how many people will say yes.

5. **LinkedIn profile:** A LinkedIn profile is a combination of a CV, cover letter, references document and a moving and living database of your network. Use it to create your own personal advertising, to search for jobs or meet new people.

6. **Facebook profile:** Millions of people have Facebook profiles, but almost no one has branded themselves properly using this medium. Be sure to include a Facebook picture of just you, while turning on the privacy options that disable the ability for people to tag you in pictures and videos.

7. **Publish something of value:** In addition to your blog posts, consider authoring a book about your expertise. It's not as difficult as it might sound (nor as easy as you think it might be), but you'll be glad you did it. Think of all the various gurus you follow on Twitter or see at conferences; they have all written at least one book.

8. **Go speak:** If you do a good job on the other bullet points here, people may want to meet you in the real world. You'll have to be more proactive here, but you should be able to find regional (and some national) events to speak at.

Communicating your brand: tools

If you're new to the concept of personal PR and how it all works, I've compiled a handy ten-step guide to getting started below:

1. **Identify your objectives:** A personal PR campaign without objectives will be doomed from the start so it's worthwhile thinking about what you really want to achieve from it and why those things are important to your business.

2. **DIY or outsource?** Running a personal PR campaign can be a full-time job and requires a lot of specialist skills such as search engine optimisation, media management and copywriting for articles and press releases; it's advisable to outsource it to a professional.

3. **Who are you targeting?** Targeting the wrong people can be very costly in terms of money and time invested in the

campaign as well as not achieving the objectives that you set out to achieve.

4. **Writing for your audience:** One of the most common mistakes in personal PR is to write articles and comments based around what you want to say, rather than what people actually want to read.

5. **Dare to be different:** If you can find a unique angle when giving comments to the press or writing for your blog, it can definitely help you get noticed, particularly in a fiercely competitive industry.

6. **Choosing the right media to get your message across:** Once you have identified your target audience you then need to reach out to them using the right media channels. This will require a lot of initial research into the best publications and websites to promote yourself on.

7. **Monitor your objectives:** There's no point in setting objectives initially if you're not going to monitor them as your campaign progresses. It's important you have the right tools in place to evaluate the activities you've undertaken.

8. **Make the most of every opportunity:** As a result of your personal PR campaign you may receive unexpected opportunities. It's important to seize any of these opportunities, such as radio and TV interviews.

9. **Use your own media to promote yourself:** There's no telling what opportunities and publicity may arise out of one of your blog posts, so using your own media such as a blog is definitely advisable as part of your overall personal PR approach.

10. **Keep your campaign going:** Many people start out on this path and fall by the wayside when they don't get instant results. If you have a well-thought-out and organised personal PR strategy you will reap the benefits if you stick with it.

Summary and next steps

Take time to digest the output of this process. Check again and make sure you have set SMART / HARD goals. Remember – always keep track. You can and must always refine your plan. You must also work hard to maintain your brand … it won't happen by itself.

Good luck!

Allan Biggar is Chairman of Allan Biggar and Company.

Banks, Businesses and Being Better Bedfellows

by Peter Ibbetson

A MIDST THE REBUILDING of business confidence following the global economic crash of 2007–8 comes one familiar phrase from businesses: "The banks aren't lending". And one familiar retort from the banks: "Businesses aren't borrowing".

Both positions are clouded by political interventions and the media's focus on whatever is the most inflammatory – usually the most pessimistic – view month by month. But even taking out the dysfunctional political and media noise, the fact remains that frequently banks and businesses appear to lack a common language.

It is no accident that most entrepreneurs would struggle to cite an ex-banker in their number, and few high street bankers are former successful entrepreneurs. Quite simply, bankers and entrepreneurs have different DNA; they think differently and act differently.

Entrepreneurs are by definition risk-takers; bankers are risk mitigators.

Yes, bankers do take risks, but in a very measured way: with an almost obsessive focus on ensuring that any losses are more than covered by surplus interest income, having made all the adjustments for capital costs, funding costs, administrative costs, etc.

These costs leave the high street banker on average with about 1% out of his margin to play with, implying that if losses are in excess of 1%, then the bank is loss-making. Putting it another way, if he gets it wrong more than one time out of a hundred, he has an unsustainable business.

This defines the way a banker looks at any lending proposition. Repayment and interest cover has to be more or less assured before a loan is made, which in turn involves a critical analysis of cash flow sensitivity and available collateral. These looking positive, he will then look to cover his position through defining clear terms and conditions on which a loan will be advanced, generally referred to as the bank covenants. Breaching these allow the banker to seek to recover his loan before the situation becomes unrecoverable.

All perfectly fair and proper through the eyes of someone responsible for looking after the depositors' money.

From an entrepreneur's viewpoint, however, such an approach is overkill. By their very nature, entrepreneurs are optimists. Frequently they risk their houses to grow their business. Instinctively they believe in what they are doing; they genuinely are convinced that repayment will be achieved as planned, and they see the role of the banker as, pure and simple, the provider of the funding they require to fulfil their business ambitions.

Frequently, however, it is equity capital that is required and not 'risk-mitigated debt', which falls outside of the appetite of a banker tied to his 1% slippage ratio. Inevitable friction then begins between a banker wishing to lend to a good viable business, and the business driven to accuse the bank of unwilling to lend on acceptable terms.

The position becomes more acute still when the business falls short of heady entrepreneurial aspiration, and is simply a 'high street SME' struggling to manage its cash flow in the face of debtors extending payment terms, not paying on time, or even just not paying at all.

This is when the definition of 'viability' is one that simply contemplates the next day, based on the bank's willingness to pay wages, rental costs and pressing creditors to stay afloat. Conversely, the banker's definition of 'viability' looks more to the 99% repayment probability, and in its absence, the availability of easily monetised collateral.

Such are the conditions that allow the development of the opposing perspectives of a bank wishing to lend to viable businesses and businesses claiming that they are unable to borrow.

Depending upon the tint of the glasses being worn, both perspectives are understandable.

Whilst in simple terms both are reasonable viewpoints, they become less so when the debate suffers from the external influences of politicians, the media and economic uncertainty as a whole. When it suits another's agenda to leverage a particular view, such as politicians keen to lay the blame for economic malaise at the door of others, very predictably they will do so. When it comes to journalists looking to gain viewer numbers and column inches by reporting selectively, or even ignorantly, they will do so.

And in both cases this becomes accentuated when there are further ingredients to add to the mix. Such issues as investment banker bonuses, LIBOR manipulation and derivative mis-selling become entwined (rightly or wrongly) in the assessment of a bank's lending appetite, and as they do a perception is created that is not necessarily representative of reality.

During the 2012–13 post-economic crisis period banks have been under acute pressure from politicians and business lobby groups to lend more freely, whist at the same time regulators have been hugely focused on ensuring the very same banks rebuild their balance sheets through strengthening their capital ratios.

Both demands have their merits in isolation, but together create a virtual impossibility.

Deeply grounded research work in early 2013 emphasised the impact of all this, with in excess of three quarters of businesses stating that they had no intention of growing their business by taking on debt. A further 7% stated that even if they did they would not contemplate approaching their bank as they believed it would be pointless. This despite extensive advertising campaigns by all the high street banks that their doors are wide open. The tendency is to believe the negative media message of 'banks closed for business', nearly half of the banks' customers being more inclined to give their opinion of their bank based, not on their own experience, but on media commentary.

The reality was that new debt to SMEs was in fact accelerating, but at the same time prepayment and general deleveraging was accelerating even faster, with the result that, on a net basis, overall lending to SMEs was declining, and as a relative, deposits by SMEs in some banks were actually in excess of borrowings.

The impact of such a consequence was that quality, viable businesses failed to invest to reinvigorate the British economy, which then began to lag competitor economies. By the end of 2012 countries such as Turkey and Mexico had more productive manufacturing sectors than the UK, with the UK broadly lagging its capital goods replacement programme by around 18 months and losing approximately £2.5 billion of annual orders which were unable to be delivered within the existing infrastructure.

At the same time demand for debt from distressed, cash-strapped businesses represented the main source of funding requests.

Higher-risk businesses borrowing, and lower risk businesses not borrowing, is not a combination that has longevity in any bank.

In an attempt to reverse this perception and stimulate the economy, the government kept interest rates low. Whilst a positive intervention for borrowers, the negative consequence saw depositors facing an erosion in the real value of their savings with minimal returns. This is tolerable by most in the short term but it is becoming a huge burden to the growing retiring population, who are faced with annuity returns that fall well short of the levels necessary to maintain living standards and facilitate discretionary spend.

The temptation has therefore been to save rather than invest, both personally and in businesses, leaving open the debate as to whether low interest rates are achieving their objective.

As was evident in the global financial crash of 2007–8 – no different in many ways from the 1930s – at the heart of economic health is confidence. In all walks of life, when confidence is lost, failure is a real possibility, but recovering confidence cannot always be easily defined. It is an intangible feel-good factor that requires momentum being built by 'the brave', before the masses follow. Only at that stage can confidence move towards optimism, and investment to recovery.

Which leads to the question of who represents 'the brave' – the businesses or the banks, the politicians or the media? And what tangible actions can be taken to regenerate the intangible confidence, without offending individual 'cast in stone' agendas.

So, taken in turn, what can each do to play their part?

It is reasonable to assume that the politicians will not vary their stance – on the one hand looking towards individual re-election, and on the other hand at achieving party re-election – of maintaining the balance between short-term vote-winning gestures and longer-term social and economic policies. Key in this is indeed recovering confidence, which in businesses' eyes is driven by stability. The most significant move here was the importing from Canada of 'forward guidance', a clear indicator that rates were to remain low for the foreseeable future. This played both to depositors and borrowers and started the recovery of the property market, and a sense that spending surplus cash and borrowing were sensible strategies.

With such clarity, the banks were able to offer medium and long-term debt at attractive pricing to those borrowers with sufficient confidence to invest.

It also revolved around a belief, or otherwise, that the banks would behave properly and professionally going forward. Trust had been almost completely undermined by what was seen and promoted in the media as 'fat cat greed' by bankers leading to the financial crash. This of course was exacerbated by various individual scandals.

The challenge the high street banks had to grapple with was that the negative perceptions levelled at them actually did not relate to them. LIBOR, swaps, bonuses, rogue traders all lived in the investment banking sides of the banks, not in the high street. But the portrayal in the media did not reflect this, nor did it afford balanced discussion on the transmission of high street banking over the previous two decades, from a local relationship to a centralised, structured template. Lost was that this transmission was driven by regulatory change, and, more so, by shareholder demands for more cost-effective models … many of the shareholders being the very businesses uneasy at the impact. Whatever the reason, it left the banks with the need for a 'trust rebuilding' programme in addition to simply providing cheap debt.

This programme, which in some shape extended across all the banks, centred around stabilising, and then enhancing, relationships, without surrendering the centralised credit risk control structure … which in truth probably helped to avoid a substantially greater number of businesses failures than had been seen in previous down-cycles, and which arguably would have been much worse had local lending discretions been retained.

Extensive liaisons with business lobby groups developed at local level; regular business surgeries were run by all the banks, and bit by bit trusted relationships began to form. New propositions, such as Bizcrowd, emerged, aimed at facilitating business opportunities between member businesses. Whole re-education programmes were established to replace, albeit at an abridged level, the former banking exams, to reassure businesses that high street bankers did actually understand banking, and the need for relationships between businesses and bankers. Some went further still, with the RBS Group putting in place obligatory secondment programmes for all its business managers, requiring them actually to work for several days each year within businesses to genuinely appreciate how businesses think and operate.

An approach by the banks, combining the relationship-rebuilding and the sensible provision of cheaply priced debt, is a reasonable response to their challenges. But the success of their recovery programme and its consequent impact on the SMEs and wider economy, relies on the media, the politicians and other external influencers being positive about, and supportive of, that approach.

The alternative is a continuance of the negativity around banks and the perpetuation of the declining appetite for quality businesses to borrow and invest in growth.

For sure, there is an imperative to maintain competition and ensure that the market is open to new entrants, but the reality is that it takes a substantial time to deliver material structural change in any industry, and banking is no different.

This draws the inevitable conclusion that it is more productive to work together as bankers, politicians, media and businesses in the rebuilding of economic confidence than it is to draw battle lines between agendas which are not necessarily aligned … but it does still leave open the question as to how the misalignments should be smoothed.

Peter Ibbetson is Chairman of Small Businesses, RBS and NatWest.

Sponsors

AXA Business Insurance

AXA Business Insurance specialises in protection for micro, small and medium-sized businesses in the UK. We are proud of the people we protect. After all, our builders, architects, plumbers and retailers are the power at the heart of the British economy.

Start-ups and established firms alike trust us to protect them and deliver peace of mind. It's easy to purchase business insurance online at **www.axa.co.uk/business** Meanwhile, shops, motor traders and surgeries (to name but a few) can call our dedicated advisors or arrange on-site visits to arrange cover.

And when the going gets really tough, our award-winning* claims service gets our customers and their communities back on their feet fast.

Our smart approach to insurance means providing free, crystal clear guidance on business risk and protection. For free news, tips and advice visit Business Guardian Angel at **www.businessguardianangel.com**

Supporting Entrepreneurship

By sponsoring the Service Industry Entrepreneur of the Year Award, we're doing our bit to engage with new talent and wave the flag for small businesses in the UK. Coming up with a good idea and launching out on your own is a brave and exciting move. At AXA Business Insurance, we want to be there with you right from the start.

*Following the 2011 riots in the UK's major cities, we were recognised with a leading industry award for the quality of support we gave to affected businesses (July 2012, British Insurance Awards, Major Losses category).

Bizcrowd

Bizcrowd is a **free** online business community that enables users to connect with other UK companies, showcase their services and expand their client base.

Creating a Bizcrowd Profile is a quick and easy way for an SME to enhance its web presence. It allows users to follow activities on sector specific Noticeboards, on which they can post business Needs or Questions, and receive post alerts and answers from others. Furthermore, companies can also benefit from a wide range of multiplatform information including industry news, business tips and success case-studies, written by the Bizcrowd Editorial Team and published on the website, Twitter and Facebook.

Bizcrowd. Where business finds business.

Dell

For more than 28 years, Dell has empowered countries, communities, customers and people everywhere to use technology to realise their dreams. Customers trust us to deliver technology solutions that help them do and achieve more, whether they're at home, work, school or anywhere in their world. Today, its goals remain the same – bringing innovative solutions to customers, doing right by them, and believing in the dreams of entrepreneurs and helping small and medium businesses grow and better serve their customers by drawing greater value from technology.

Dell has a number of programmes aimed at empowering entrepreneurs, start-ups and small businesses worldwide to support every stage of a growing business. As part of its commitment to supporting women entrepreneurs, Dell established the Dell Women's Entrepreneur Network (DWEN) as part of its wider Women Powering Business community which actively engages with over 2,000 women worldwide with the goal of accelerating opportunities for women business leaders to expand their networks, find valuable resources and showcase how technology can enable business innovation and growth.

Learn more about Dell's support for entrepreneurs and its business technology solutions by visiting: **www.dell.co.uk/business** or following **@dellsmbuk** on Twitter.

Exact

And it all comes together.

Exact is a leading global supplier of financial and business software. The company develops industry-specific on-premise and cloud solutions for manufacturing, wholesale and distribution, professional services and accountancy businesses.

Our software, Exact Online, combines these solutions in one online system. All the critical performance information you need is available in real-time on an easy to understand, personalised dashboard. It means businesses can look at their numbers differently and do more. We call it Big Picture Business Software. Over 100,000 European companies already use Exact Online.

Whether you simply need online accounts, or broader functions such as time and billing, project management, inventory, stock management, CRM and more, it's all possible with Exact Online's cloud, mobile and app-driven solutions.

Kaspersky Lab

The company today

Kaspersky Lab is an international group operating in almost 200 countries and territories worldwide. The company is headquartered in Moscow, Russia, with its holding company registered in the United Kingdom.

Kaspersky Lab currently employs over 2,800 highly qualified specialists. It has 30 representative territory offices in 29 countries and its products and technologies provide protection for over 300 million users and over 250,000 corporate clients worldwide. The company provides a wide range of products and solutions for different types of clients, with a special focus on large enterprises, and small and medium-sized businesses.

Over 300 million people worldwide are protected by Kaspersky Lab products and technologies. Kaspersky Lab's corporate client base exceeds 250,000 companies located around the globe, ranging from small and medium-sized businesses all the way up to large governmental and commercial organizations. Kaspersky Lab's customer retention index is significantly higher than the industry average and those for key competitors: 106 for corporate products and 99 for consumer products in 2012.**

**TNS consumer retention survey 2012.

XLN

XLN is the small business specialist.

We are a leading supplier of business services to small businesses in the UK, with over 130,000 small business customers across the UK.

Simply, we provide business phone lines, business broadband, mobile, gas, electricity and card processing to the SME sector.

XLN was founded by Christian Nellemann in 2002. Christian was Ernst & Young's Entrepreneur of the Year for Technology and Communication in 2006, winning again in 2010. In 2010 and 2011 XLN also won British Venture Capital Association (BVCA) awards for 'Best Private Equity Backed Management Team'.

XLN has been a National Business Awards Finalist for 6 years: 2004, 2005, 2006, 2009, 2010 and 2012. In 2007 and 2008, XLN was ranked on the Sunday Times Tech Track 100 survey of the 100 fastest growing technology companies: in 2011 and 2012 XLN was listed in the *Sunday Times* Buyout Track 100 and in 2011, 2012 and 2013 was listed in the *Sunday Times* Profit Track top 100.

More details at: **www.xln.co.uk**

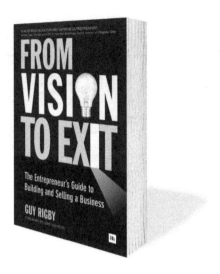

A high-growth success story

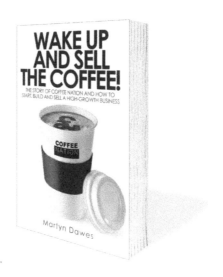

Martyn Dawes set out to build a high-growth business with a simple idea and the will to do whatever was required to make it a success.

Twelve years later he sold this business – Coffee Nation – for £23m.

Through the course of an exciting narrative, Martyn shares his experiences of growing a business and his knowledge of what you should and shouldn't do.

Mistakes to avoid are revealed just as honestly as the good decisions, making this is an unusually frank and valuable account for anyone looking to build their own business.

WWW.HARRIMAN-HOUSE.COM/ WAKEUPANDSELLTHECOFFEE

The UK's leading business content partner

Creating bespoke books, eBooks and apps

For businesses big and small

Harriman House is a content producer specialising in business and finance. We publish our own range of print and digital products and also offer our unique high quality services to corporate clients, working with them to produce a range of bespoke content solutions. Get in touch now to find the right solution for you!

SOLUTIONS.HARRIMAN-HOUSE.COM